Praise for *Being Professiona*

"Storytelling, and more importantly, building, at its finest. I picked up Coplan's book thinking I knew much. He knows the little details and big ideas that matter. Indispensable."
—**Dave Watson**, editor, Movies Matter

"Whether you are writing your first or twentieth screenplay, Adam Coplan's *Being Professional* should be on every scriptwriter's bookshelf. Filled with sage advice from his decades of working in the film industry, Coplan touches on all areas of the craft, including defining and creating conflict, and mastering the finer points of editing. One of my favorite segments regards the Seven Vital Questions, which teaches scribes how to write more powerful scenes. And if that weren't enough, Coplan has added his tried-and-true writing exercises at the end of each chapter to help keep you on track!"
—**Kathie Fong Yoneda**, seminar leader, consultant, author, *The Script-Selling Game*

"Adam has taken his considerable experience in script development and made it readily available to anyone who has the dream of writing for a living in Hollywood."
—**David Greathouse**, executive producer, *Hacksaw Ridge*, *The Night Manager* (TV miniseries)

"The book I wish someone had written when I was a baby writer. It would have saved me a lot of trouble. If you plan on making a career out of screenwriting, this is the only place to start."
—**Jason Fuchs**, screenwriter, *Wonder Woman*, *Pan*, *Ice Age: Continental Drift*

"In a time where screenwriting seemingly is getting more and more complicated, Adam Coplan's book brings it all wonderfully back to the basics: Three-Act Structure, Character Development, Dialogue, etc. The basics that still stand the test of time."
—**Matthew Terry**, filmmaker, screenwriter, teacher

"*Being Professional* is a must-read for any aspiring screenwriter. In plain English, Adam Coplan demystifies the storytelling process, laying out guidelines from basic structure to the abstracts that can turn a good story into a great script. By referencing recent film favorites, this book offers countless pointers for beginning screenwriters, and some excellent reminders for veterans as well. Bravo, Adam! And from a generation of filmgoers, thanks for writing it!"
—**Scott Williams**, writer, executive producer, *NCIS*, *Castle*, *Bones*

"*Being Professional* not only explains every single aspect of screen-writing in a direct, precise, and concise way, but also illustrates the do's and don'ts with tons of old and recent movies. Its essential tips and writing exercises make it an excellent guide for teachers and anyone interested in writing film."
—**Marcela Toledo**, journalist, writer, editor, producer, translator

"Developing a professional-looking script is half the battle in being a screenwriter. Adam Coplan's *Being Professional* walks you through all the different elements you need to consider to make your script look professional."
—**Tom Farr**, writer, teacher, storyteller

Being
Professional

– A MASTER GUIDE TO THE DO'S AND DON'TS OF SCREENWRITING –

Adam Coplan

MICHAEL WIESE PRODUCTIONS

Published by Michael Wiese Productions
12400 Ventura Blvd. #1111
Studio City, CA 91604
(818) 379-8799, (818) 986-3408 (FAX)
mw@mwp.com
www.mwp.com

Cover design by Johnny Ink. www.johnnyink.com
Interior design by William Morosi
Illustrations by Daniel Oviedo. Portfolio and contact at daniel34.jimdo.com
Copyediting by Ross Plotkin
Printed by McNaughton & Gunn

Manufactured in the United States of America

Library of Congress Cataloging-in-Publication Data

Names: Coplan, Adam, 1972-
Title: Being professional : a master guide to the do's and don'ts of
  screenwriting / Adam Coplan.
Description: Studio City, CA : Published by Michael Wiese Productions, [2016]
Identifiers: LCCN 2016008723 | ISBN 9781615932498
Subjects: LCSH: Motion picture authorship--Handbooks, manuals, etc.
Classification: LCC PN1996 .C81425 2016 | DDC 808.2/3--dc23
LC record available at https://lccn.loc.gov/2016008723

Printed on Recycled Stock

For my mother,
who pleaded with me as a child to
turn off the television and read a book.

I never listened so it's only fitting I am now a published author.

Table of Contents

Foreword

BY MATT BERENSON

I am a film and TV producer who has worked in the entertainment industry for 25 years, and produced 15 films since 1999 with several more in the pipeline. I have worked with screenwriters developing their (or my) ideas from scratch; I have also worked with screenwriters who hand me an original screenplay to help them make it the best it can possibly be; and, I've even taken a stab at writing myself, which helped me understand in a more real way all the challenges writers face in trying to tell their story. As a producer, I am looking for screenwriters with a voice, with great ideas, with an understanding of the craft of screenwriting, with a strong work ethic, and last, with an understanding that they work in a collaborative medium. A screenwriter's job is to provide the initial inspiration for a film, to bring their characters to life, create a solid structure for the story they are telling, and ultimately to provide a strong blueprint for a film or TV series.

However, if they want to be successful, they must also understand and accept that the financier, the producer(s), the director, the actors, and the rest of the creative team all play significant roles in turning their blueprint into the finished product, which will inevitably evolve from what they originally envisioned. For example, as anyone who has ever made a film before can attest, the final "rewrite" is done in postproduction by the director and editor. Things as fundamental as the beginning or ending of the film can change in post. If you are not comfortable with this, then you should either a) not be a screenwriter, or b) work towards becoming a writer/director like Quentin Tarantino or the Coen Brothers, who are truly the authors of their films. And even they have to learn to collaborate with others.

Here's what I'm not looking for: writers who don't understand that screenwriting is a craft that has to be studied and learned through repeated viewings of their favorite films, with lots of "practice" (and by that I mean failing many times before they succeed) and from reading books like this that will help them avoid the pitfalls of the amateur and become a working professional in the industry. I'm also not looking to work with writers who are lazy or precious or entitled (although who is?). Just to clarify what I mean by "precious," I'm not talking about intelligently defending your ideas or creative choices; I'm talking about not being willing to listen, about letting insecurity and/or ego get in the way of a better idea (no matter who or where it may come from).

Lastly, I'm not looking to work with writers who think screenwriting is a quick and easy way to fame and fortune. Instead, I'm looking for screenwriters who love film and television as much as I do; who are obsessed with the story they want to tell; and who are willing to work hard to get there, writing multiple drafts (sometimes for free) until a talented filmmaker, financier, and/or bankable actor can clearly see and understand their vision for the film and feel the passion behind it. If you're the next Aaron Sorkin, fame and fortune will come. But screenwriting has to be your calling, first and foremost. If you can imagine doing anything else, then you probably shouldn't pursue a career as a screenwriter. It's too competitive and too difficult for the casual fan who thinks they may have a good idea for a movie (which they probably don't).

And that brings me to my final words of wisdom for anyone reading this book. We live in an increasingly global marketplace for screen stories, a marketplace in which China will soon be the global box office leader and number one consumer of film. When I started in the film business 25 years ago, 70% of worldwide box office came from the U.S. Now, the opposite is true. Westerns, films about baseball, or urban films like *Boyz n the Hood* (a hit when I started in the business) are getting increasingly difficult to make, because they don't "travel." Does that mean that every one of your ideas has to have the potential to be a global tent pole? Of course not. Does it mean that you should pay attention to what is doing well around the world and not just in the United States? To quote the legendary studio mogul and producer Robert Evans, "You bet it does."

It is rare to find insight and instruction from someone with so much experience "in the room" where script and film decisions are made, and such a thorough understanding of the industry perspective that is so often lost in more academic or speculative offerings. This book boasts a practicality that will be an asset to anyone who is serious not just about screenwriting, but screenwriting as a serious profession. I highly recommend it!

Good luck, dear reader and aspiring screenwriter. Whatever you do, don't give up on your dreams!

MATT BERENSON *is a producer whose films include* Daddy Day Care, *starring Eddie Murphy;* The Place Beyond the Pines, *starring Ryan Gosling and Bradley Cooper; and the recent hit horror film* The Boy, *from Hollywood's newest studio, STX Entertainment.*

A Few Introductory Thoughts...

While there are many lessons contained within the pages of this text, a few basic truths should be understood before you proceed.

The process of learning to be a working screenwriter is not one that should be taken lightly. Many presume it is easy to write a screenplay, and therefore they can do it with little or no advance preparation. As with any skill or art form, it takes practice, passion, and tremendous dedication. Would you expect to hit a home run the first time you step in a batter's box? What if it was in Yankee Stadium? That's the naiveté of presuming you can write Leonardo DiCaprio's next movie having never even written a scene, let alone a full script before.

While this textbook is applicable and worthwhile to all screenwriters, the contents are specifically geared towards spec screenwriting, begging the question: What is a spec? According to the dictionary...

> **"... made, built, or done with hopes of but no assurance of payment or sale; without commitment by a client or buyer."**

Of the approximately 50,000 scripts registered with the Writers Guild each year, the vast majority of these are specs. It's what you'll write as you endeavor to gain recognition and a paycheck in the industry. Though established screenwriters will often forego selling a pitch or writing on assignment in favor of writing a spec, they have representation and have achieved a level of credibility that affords them freedoms and considerations that you have not yet earned. What does this mean? First and foremost, that in addition to superior content, you have the added challenge of needing to craft a seamless, effortless read to thwart the gatekeepers who are predisposed to stop early, skim, and above all else, reject your work.

Another critical point is that no matter how brilliant, innovative, or original the idea is, your bout of inspiration is only a launching pad, a far cry from the complete script you will need to garner attention or remuneration for your work. The initial light bulb moment NEVER provides someone the middle of a movie or the subtle nuances of both story and character. NOBODY ever conceives 100 or more pages in one astounding thought. You MUST outline if you hope to have any success. Professionals outline... Do you really believe you don't need to?

When you forego outlining (and this may sound familiar to many) you will excitedly tear through the first 20 or 30 pages before you slam into a brick wall, at a loss about how to bridge the gap to your Climax and the resolution of your core conflict. The Second Act is the meat of your movie and NEVER part of the original idea. Outlining is far and away, the surest method to crack this section and deliver a fully formed feature script, worthy of production.

There is a vast array of screenwriting books available to advise, educate, and inspire you. As with guides on any subject, some are better than others. I will let you be the judge of where this book fits among them, but what I do wish to address is the particular issue I have with those guides or methods that claim the ability to boil screenwriting down to a checklist or series of simple steps.

Established and professional screenwriters can benefit greatly from many of the lessons in these books because their experience allows them to pick and choose the tips and tools that will work for them, while disregarding the rest. Novice and aspiring screenwriters all too often take these simplified models and follow them with extreme rigidity. This robs screenwriters of their artistic expression and creative spark. You cannot teach someone how to paint like Picasso by giving them a book of paint by numbers. That isn't art and if you aspire to be a professional screenwriter, you are, like it or not, an aspiring artist. It requires talent, passion, and a desire to engage and entertain an audience. Take the lessons contained within this text to heart and employ them in your work, but make sure something of you remains in your writing for that is your best weapon in your ensuing battle for success.

One of the most important lessons is to recognize that screen-writing is unique as a writing medium in that every other type, from a greeting card or poem to a novel or magazine article, are all meant to be read. Screenplays MUST be written visually as they are intended to be viewed on a screen. We'll delve further into how this is done later, but for now, the key is to recognize that your intended audience is watching your words, NOT reading them.

You MUST never lose sight of this as film is a visual experience and the script is the foundation of that. The fact that you are reading this suggests you are interested in expanding your understanding of the subject and working to improve.

Congratulations... this dramatically increases your likelihood of success!

Finally, a screenplay is a literary blueprint for a collaborative process. As the screenwriter, you are the first person to engage in that process by devising a story and putting words to paper, but you are by no means the last. You've all seen the very long list of names in the credits at the beginning and end of a movie. Whether it is the director who will have significant input, the producers and studio executives who will oversee and guide the process, or the actors who will breathe life into your char-acters, you must understand that many different people with a variety of jobs and responsibilities will contribute to shape the final product. That cannot scare or deter you if you wish to be successful.

In truth, it is something you must fully embrace for those who enter this world with a hands-off approach, believing the script is their private domain and therefore only theirs to manipulate, are destined for great disappointment.

Embrace your role in the process and you will be far more likely to remain involved to see your voice, your words, and your vision realized on screen.

CHAPTER 1

Three Act Structure…
It's Not the Enemy

The standard measure for screenwriting is 1 page = 1 minute of screen time.

Therefore, a 120 page script = a 2 hour movie.

The First Act	20–30 pages
The Second Act	50–60 pages
The Third Act	20–30 pages
TOTAL	90–120 pages

The variance in these numbers is often attributable to genre beyond any other factor. Faster paced films like action, comedy, and horror tend to be shorter than dramas, which due to character demands may require greater detail and length. Kids have limited attention spans so family films are generally kept on the shorter side as well. True stories, historical epics, and many science fiction/fantasy films often run longer thanks to a higher degree of detail, a need to include an origin story, or more time spent establishing an original, newly imagined world.

Budget can also play a role so particularly for those of you intending to shoot independently, be mindful that every page substantially increases the overall cost of a film's production. On paper, it may not seem like a big deal, but an extra 10 minutes of screen time could mean

tens of thousands to millions more on your budget and even the difference between getting a film made and never seeing it come to fruition.

A clear understanding of these benchmarks is crucial as far too
often, scripts get submitted with First Acts that end in the 50s or
Second Acts that are half as long as they should be. As you progress through this text, it will become clearer why that is such a
monumental flaw.

THE FIRST ACT

The PROTAGONIST or main character: Who is he, she, or it?

- Introduce your main characters and what connects them to one
  another.
  1. Are they friends or enemies?
  2. Are they strangers?
  3. Is there an attraction?
  4. What dynamics exist between them?

- The SETTING: Where and when is the story taking place?
  1. What time period? The Bronze Age, 1954, the Great Depres-
     sion, A Long Time Ago in a Galaxy Far, Far Away, Yesterday,
     etc....
  2. What location(s)? Milwaukee, Mars, Middle Earth, etc....
  3. Is it a real place or one born of fantasy?

An additional point to consider regarding setting: **How will it
impact the tone?** Disneyland in the summer FEELS very different than
Transylvania in the winter.

Along the same lines, recognize that locations can in many ways
become like a character in your story. Having a city or place come
alive in your script is a great way to add atmosphere and substantially enhance your work, e.g. the romance of Paris, the desolation
of a desert, the lurid sexuality of Rio de Janeiro, and so forth. Given
that one of your primary responsibilities in the First Act is to set a

mood and engage your audience, be mindful of how you might use the setting to assist in accomplishing this.

It can be obvious such as in films like *Casablanca*, *Fargo*, or even *Avatar*. In other cases, it's a major component of the premise such as in *Beverly Hills Cop*, a fish out of water story placing a Detroit street cop in the bizarre world of posh 90210. In *Mr. Smith Goes to Washington*, the grandeur and history of the capital is put to great effect, reflecting the struggle of Jimmy Stewart's character as he attempts to remain stalwart and true in the face of greed and political graft.

Sometimes, it is simply about employing devices such as weather, an activity, or even the time of day to create a mood.

Day is safer and happier than night. Rain is more somber than sunshine and a trip to the ballpark is as American as apple pie! The bottom line is not to forget to make the setting work to the betterment of your overall screenplay and particularly in establishing the tone of your work.

The process of outlining begins with the 7 major plot points of any script employing Three Act Structure. Identifying these benchmark moments provides key elements of your story and makes it much easier to fill in the blanks in between. Additionally, your initial idea will likely include 1 or 2 of them, which will help get you started.

MAJOR PLOT POINTS

1. The Inciting Incident
2. The First Act Break
3. An Early Complication
4. The Midpoint

5. The Second Act Break
6. The Climax
7. The Denouement
(optional)

An important note with regards to these plot points is that while many if not most are single scenes, they can and often are sequences of two or more in succession. As an example, while the Climax in *Jerry Maguire* is the single scene where Tom Cruise tells Renée Zellweger that she completes him, the Climax in *The Rock* begins with the confrontation that kills Ed Harris and runs all the way through the bombing of the island and Sean Connery pulling Nic Cage out of San Francisco Bay.

Understanding this fact will alleviate some of the pressure you might otherwise put on yourselves while trying to force your plot points into single scenes when in many cases, a sequence may be a better fit. Not that it should be emulated, but the Denouement in *Lord of the Rings: Return of the King* is 45 minutes long!

PLOT POINT #1 – THE INCITING INCIDENT

Sometimes referred to as the Setup or the Dramatic Premise.

What event takes place to set the drama in motion?

It will generally occur at roughly the midpoint of Act 1 (page 8–15), though it could be anywhere in the first 15–20 pages, including the opening scene as it was in *The Breakfast Club*. In that film, the Inciting Incident is the five kids arriving at school for Saturday detention. Their presence together sets the drama of that movie in motion.

In the case of the aforementioned *Beverly Hills Cop*, the Inciting Incident is the murder of Axel's friend in Detroit. It's why he travels to Beverly Hills and is the event that propels the story forward. In *Gladiator*, it is the moment when Marcus Aurelius tells his son that he will be succeeded by Maximus and not him. It is this action that causes Commodus to murder his father and betray the General.

A final example would be the Army's discovery in *Saving Private Ryan* that all but one of the Ryan brothers has been killed and General Marshall declares that the sole surviving brother is going to be found and sent home.

PLOT POINT #2 – THE FIRST ACT BREAK

Sometimes referred to as the Hook or the Dramatic Situation.

What are the circumstances by which the protagonist engages the core conflict of the story, setting up the drama that will exist all the way through to its eventual resolution, whether they are triumphant or not?

The First Act Break is always the final scene or sequence of the First Act. It is the introduction of the core conflict of the film. Your protagonist facing this conflict IS your movie, regardless of whether they prove successful in the endeavor.

Their engagement of the conflict is also what transitions the story from Act 1 into the Second Act. When people ask what a movie is about... The conflict engaged in the First Act Break would be the bulk of any competent answer.

Some examples... In *The Breakfast Club*, the First Act Break is their assignment to each write an essay explaining who they are. Discovering that despite their apparent differences, they are all very much the same is the lesson they each learn. In *The Hangover*, the Wolf Pack going in search of Doug, their missing friend, is the First Act Break. In the case of *Raiders of the Lost Ark*, Indiana Jones goes in search of the ark. It is this very straightforward action that bridges Acts 1 and 2 and ignites the drama the rest of the way.

The Inciting Incident sets up a conflict and the First Act Break is your protagonist engaging that conflict. In *Saving Private Ryan*, only one Ryan brother is left alive, so Tom Hanks and his ranger team being assigned and assuming the task of finding and safely extracting him becomes the core conflict and thus the First Act Break.

For this reason, it is also sometimes referred to as a Call To Action, though I tend to avoid that moniker, as it doesn't always seem an appropriate label. This scene or sequence establishes the core conflict of your film and the struggle to resolve it is the "meat" of your movie. The obstacles that stand in the protagonist's way will largely comprise your Second Act while the eventual resolution of the conflict, successful or not, will dominate the Third Act.

The Inciting Incident and First Act Break tend to be the two plot points that are a part of a screenwriter's original idea. This is why people who don't outline typically speed through a rough first act before hitting a brick wall. They have the setup and main character in their heads, but once they've reached Act 2, they have no idea what comes next or how to fill that so called "meat" of the movie. Taking the time to figure that out via outlining makes busting through that wall infinitely easier and far more pleasurable. GUARANTEED!

THE SECOND ACT

The Second Act is all about challenges. Specifically, it is about the many obstacles that stand in the way of your protagonist achieving a resolution of the core conflict. Whether that conflict is about curing a disease, discovering the identity of a killer, falling in love, or defeating the Joker, your Second Act is where your protagonist will fight to advance towards a positive resolution to the core conflict. Making these challenges a true test, thus forcing your protagonist to risk and struggle, is what will ultimately make for a satisfying film. If success comes too quickly or easily, who do you expect will fork over the cash to make your story the focus of their Friday or Saturday night?

PLOT POINT #3 – AN EARLY COMPLICATION

The Second Act must have consistent escalations with emotional peaks and valleys to manipulate the audience's emotions, thus maintaining their interest.

The first such beat comes in the form of an Early Complication, which is typically a valley and occurs in the first 10–15 pages of Act 2.

The First Act Break is generally a positive moment of forward progress and so it only stands to reason that the next major event has the opposite effect. This will generally take the form of an obstacle or challenge that prevents further progress, at least in the short term. It can also be an event or circumstance that makes the resolution of the core conflict, suddenly more difficult than ever before.

A perfect example of an Early Complication is in the film *Back to the Future*. Marty has found Doc Brown and together, they are moving forward with a plan to send him home. However, things become infinitely more complicated when Marty inadvertently gets in the way of his parent's first meeting, which in turn led to their falling in love and eventually getting married and having children, including Marty. Even worse, his own mother now has a crush on him! So, in addition to getting home, he must fix the past and shift her affection back where it belongs, thus restoring his parent's marriage and guaranteeing his future existence.

Occasionally, the Early Complication is a bit more elaborate and involves a step forward prior to several steps back. In cases such as this, the Early Complication is often referred to as the **First Culmination**.

It is exemplified by a moment of apparent victory where it will seem, either to the protagonist, the audience, or both, that the main character is on the verge of success with regards to the core conflict, however they will come up just short. It is then closely followed by a major setback that has the effect of making resolution of the core conflict significantly harder than had previously been envisioned.

A First Culmination allows you to craft both a peak and a valley in the same scene or sequence. As attractive as that may sound, only employ it if it makes sense for your specific story. The example from *Back to the Future* is a brilliant obstacle and one you could argue is the best from a fantastic film. Sometimes more complicated isn't better, it's just more. An Early Complication is a must, but having it be a First Culmination is not.

Jerry Maguire employed a First Culmination. Tom Cruise had been fired and started his own firm at the end of Act 1. Maguire's first priority is to hang on to Jerry O'Connell's character, a college quarterback who is about to go at the top of the NFL draft, guaranteeing a lucrative contract and a juicy, seven-figure commission for his agent. Jerry thinks he's successfully done this, only to discover on the eve of the draft that he's been dumped in favor of his former colleague, protégé, and now arch rival. Instead of representing the number 1 pick, cashing in an easy commission, and moving forward without missing a beat, he's left humiliated, financially strapped, and desperate.

In *Midnight Run*, Robert De Niro is a bounty hunter hired to find Charles Grodin's fugitive accountant. He locates him easily, but if he's able to transport him from New York to Los Angeles quickly, there's no movie. Upon boarding the plane, Grodin's character feigns craziness and gets them tossed off the jet. Instead of a simple flight east to west, they must now travel cross country the long way and De Niro must contend with a series of challenges aimed at preventing his successful return.

PLOT POINT #4 – THE MIDPOINT

The Midpoint roughly occurs (no surprise) at the midpoint of Act 2 and of the script as a whole. It is a moment where the stakes change, often becoming more dangerous or risky, depending on the genre. This plot point is generally more pronounced in proactive genres like action and horror because the stakes are more evident and the cost of failure less obscure. Sometimes it is simply the reveal of new information that complicates matters. Perhaps it is the revelation of a ticking clock, which builds tension and suspense. It could be the delivery of a harrowing diagnosis or perhaps a key character dies. What it absolutely MUST be is a dynamic moment halfway through your story that builds the audience's interest, elevates the stakes, and settles them into their seats for the second half of the film. It aims to keep their focus on the screen and not on their watches!

In *Top Gun*, Goose's death is the Midpoint that dramatically alters the course of events. In *The Rock*, the massacre of the SEAL team leaves Cage and Connery alone to deal with the threat to San Francisco. In *Gladiator*, the Midpoint occurs when Maximus reveals himself to the Emperor in the Coliseum, swearing he will have his revenge.

In *The Matrix*, some might argue that the Midpoint is when Neo meets with the Oracle and she tells him he isn't the one. A case could be made, but I believe it is the scene when Cypher is eating steak with Agent Smith and discussing his deal to betray Morpheus and the others. Not only does this scene occur right at the actual midpoint of the film, it substantially elevates the tension as the group enters the matrix to see the Oracle shortly thereafter.

As previously stated, the Midpoint may be subtler in less proactive genres. For example, in *Big*, Tom Hanks goes on a date and sleeps with Elizabeth Perkins. This affects his thinking and for the balance of Act 2, he loses sight of his goal to return to his childlike self. It is the moment where he begins to question whether he truly wants to return to his youthful existence rather than remain an adult. Love and sex can often have that type of effect.

The Midpoint may be the least obvious plot point when the outlining process begins. It will NEVER be part of the original concept. That said, its presence is vital as one of the pivotal peaks or valleys necessary for a successful Second Act. It is also a time when your audience will either be contemplating a bathroom run or conversely, have their attention further engaged by the world you have created. Work to conceive a game-changing moment that will build your audience's interest in the balance of the film.

PLOT POINT #5 – THE SECOND ACT BREAK

The end of the Second Act is generally marked by the protagonist's emotional low point. They have hit a wall and all hope of success APPEARS to be lost. The suggestion of surrender will likely be present, however that's highly unlikely as then the movie would be over as well. Perhaps the conflict feels insurmountable and they cannot continue. It is often triggered by the loss of something or someone crucial to the resolution of the core conflict. The protagonist choosing to soldier on in the face of such an emotional low point is what propels the story forward into Act 3.

Such is the case in *An Officer and a Gentleman* where Sid's suicide prompts Mayo's subsequent decision to drop out. Another example is in *The Shawshank Redemption*. It begins with Tommy's revelation of the real killer of Andy's wife, followed by the warden sending Andy to solitary for a month, and finally, Tommy's murder.

A prime example stemming instead from character development is the powerful and highly entertaining scene from *The Breakfast Club* where the five kids each reveal their vulnerabilities to each other. Emilio Estevez wishes his knee would blow out, Anthony Michael Hall was contemplating suicide, Ally Sheedy is achingly lonely, Judd Nelson is abused, and Molly Ringwald is drowning under the pressure from her parents, her friends, and herself. Suddenly these five very different characters feel bonded by their shared sadness and fears.

The betrayal of William Wallace and of all the Scots by Robert the Bruce in *Braveheart* is that film's sad Second Act Break and another prime example.

THIS IS VERY IMPORTANT! In the case of a film that has a sad or tragic ending that is the emotional low point, The Second Act Break reverses tonally with the Climax and becomes the emotional high point of the script. In such cases, the audience is teased with the possibility of success, rather than failure.

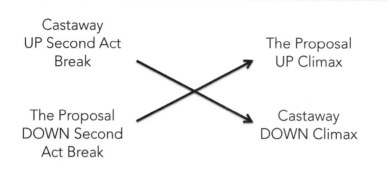

This graphic represents that tonal shift. For example, in *The Proposal*, the Climax is a happy one during which Sandra Bullock and Ryan Reynolds wind up in love and together. As such, the Second Act Break is necessarily the opposite. It's an emotionally down moment where Bullock confesses her actions at the altar rather than marry under false pretenses and resolves herself to being deported. The audience is teased with the possibility that they won't wind up together.

Conversely, the film *Castaway* has a sad ending. Tom Hanks has survived years of being marooned only to make it home and discover that his true love is lost and unable to resume their relationship because of her new family. It may not be a tragic ending, but the core conflict is only partially resolved. As a result, the Second Act Break must be an emotional high. In this case, it's Hanks being rescued at sea and the end to his very lengthy ordeal.

A couple of additional examples of this emotional shift between the Second Act Break and the Climax are the films *Gladiator* and *Man on Fire*. In the former, the Second Act Break falls when Maximus agrees to a deal that will see him released and free to return at the head of an army that in addition to his personal revenge will allow him to realize the last wishes of Marcus Aurelius. It is a moment of hope that is diminished by Maximus's death in the Climax.

In *Man on Fire*, Denzel Washington exacts revenge on everyone involved in Dakota Fanning's murder until, in the Second Act Break, he discovers she's not actually dead. His hope is reignited, as suddenly, the young girl he loves may actually be alive. Though she is successfully rescued, the film has an emotionally low ending because Washington's character dies to get her back.

THE THIRD ACT

The Third Act is when your various characters and subplots converge and all are brought to some form of resolution. It is common for any lingering fractures among important characters to be mended so that they may band together if need be, or to bring the protagonist to full strength as he or she engages the Climax. Proactive steps are taken to finally overcome the challenges presented by your core conflict and bring forth an ending that is satisfying for the audience.

PLOT POINT #6 – THE CLIMAX

Perhaps the most obvious of the major plot points to identify, the Climax is the resolution of the core conflict. It is the point at which the plot reaches maximum tension and the forces in opposition confront each other at a peak of physical or emotional tension.

In relationship films, the resolution between the characters will often be the Climax as the core conflict is the relationship itself. Examples of this include *Pretty Woman*, *When Harry Met Sally…*, and *Say Anything*.

Critical! Do not ever forget that the First Act Break and the Climax MUST match one another. One is the setup of the core conflict and the other is the resolution of said conflict. If they do not match, your script won't make any sense and will not go any further. **GUARANTEED**!

I'm often asked for an example to illustrate this and I don't have one. Because of all the mistakes that are made throughout the development process, this one will NEVER make it to a screen. This mistake can't be made. It is occasionally seen in poorly written screenplays, but when it occurs, the script is quickly rejected.

The closest example I can give is in the execution of *The Matrix* trilogy. If you look at all three films as the beginning, middle, and end of a larger story, which they are, you'll see that the first film, an absolutely brilliant movie, sets up the core conflict of needing to free humanity from the computers. However, the Climax of the third film involves Neo inexplicably battling an infinite number of Agent Smiths rather than a final confrontation to free humanity. Moreover, the film basically ends with humans in the same position they were in at the outset of the first movie. It is this failure that ultimately was the downfall of these films as a trilogy, despite the undisputed greatness of the first installment.

PLOT POINT #7 – THE DENOUEMENT

The Denouement is in most films, but not all. It is the calm after the storm so to speak. Often, after the Climax, there are loose threads that need tending. In other cases, it is simply an opportunity for humor such as in *The Hangover* when the audience sees the hilarious and revealing pictures taken during the forgotten night in Vegas.

In the *Star Trek* reboot, the Climax is the confrontation and final battle with Nero. Afterwards, in the Denouement, we return to Starfleet to see Kirk's promotion, followed by the assumption of his command and his acceptance of Spock as his first officer.

The Lord of the Rings: Return of the King has what may be the longest Denouement in film history. The Hobbits and other surviving members of the Fellowship reunite at Frodo's bedside, then Aragorn's coronation, the return to the shire, Sam's marriage, finishing the book, and ultimately Frodo leaving with Gandalf and Elrond. This is the rare extreme and not something to be emulated.

Most films do possess a Denouement, but you are best served sticking to just a few minutes and recognizing that anything north of 10 is likely a terrible mistake.

Some movies and/or scripts end with the Climax, in which case, there is no Denouement. An example of this is *Dead Poets Society*. Ethan Hawke stands on his desk and declares, "O Captain, my Captain" to a defeated Robin Williams. Josh Charles and several others soon follow his brave lead. It is a dramatic and enormously satisfying Climax that leaves no need for additional scenes. The movie is over. *Pretty Woman* is another example. The Climax is Edward and Vivian kissing on the fire escape. It's also the end of the movie.

Once again, here are the 7 major plot points.

1. The Inciting Incident
2. The First Act Break
3. An Early Complication
4. The Midpoint
5. The Second Act Break
6. The Climax
7. The Denouement (optional)

When outlining, begin with these scenes or sequences. Even the simplest kernel of an idea will typically include the first two. Ask yourself how you want the film to end. What resolution do you want for your setup? Happy, sad, tragic, etc.... This should provide a sense of the Climax. As you begin to expand your outline and plot your Second Act, the others will come into clearer focus.

It is vital you remember that screenwriting is a fluid medium. It requires rewriting; no draft will be a final draft until the film is actually wrapped, and even then changes and/or additions may be necessary. If you write 17 drafts and believe there is literally not a single thing left to change before the script sells to Paramount, be prepared for the studio's very first act which will be to give you notes not for draft 18, but for what they now consider to be draft 2. They're starting from scratch and couldn't care less how many versions you wrote before they handed you a check.

Don't get married to any single idea as you don't want to close yourself off to a better one later. Students are often resistant to filling in their outlines because they want it to be perfect before they put pen to paper. Do the opposite. Put every idea down and see what works. You can always change it later. Human nature prompts us to typically move forward with our first idea, but is it really so unlikely that with a little effort and creativity, you're not only capable, but likely to come up with something better? Be open to the possibilities... All of them!

ONE FINAL VERY IMPORTANT POINT...

It is likely that better than 95% of films follow the Three Act Structure. Many new writers, enamored with the most artistic of filmmakers, believe conforming to the Three Act Structure is somehow lacking in artistic merit. This could not be further from the truth, as one has nothing to do with the other. The greatest filmmakers in history regularly use and have used this structure to tell the most artistic and compelling of stories. It isn't about the structure, but making the content of your film innovative and compelling.

You are welcome to use whatever structure you want, as you are the screenwriter and the script is yours to conceive and execute. However, it is crucial that you LEARN THE RULES BEFORE YOU BREAK THEM and recognize that change, when it isn't necessary or supported by a clear purpose, is a waste of time that generally will have negative results.

KEYS TO REMEMBER

- Professional screenwriter is a highly paid and highly sought-after position. It is neither easy nor something to be entered into casually or lightly, not if you wish to be taken seriously. You're wasting your time if you believe otherwise.

- Professionals outline. Only amateurs with little, if any chance of success, forego this critical step.

- Screenwriting, unlike any other form of writing, is meant to be watched, not read. You must write visually to be a successful screenwriter.

- You must recognize that screenwriting is one part of a collaborative process, which means you cannot be resistant to change, and in fact must be open to any and all possibilities. Notes aren't a hostile act. If you can't abide your art being shaped in some part by others, become a sculptor.

- You must be aware of act breaks with regards to length. A First Act that doesn't end until page 50 or a Second Act of only 30 pages is unacceptable from a professional. The movie doesn't truly begin until your protagonist engages the core conflict in the First Act Break. The longer it takes for that to happen, the less invested a reader and/or viewer will be.

- The Second Act Break and the Climax are tonal opposites. Without this, the emotional ride for your reader won't be particularly engaging.

- The First Act Break and the Climax MUST match. The conflict resolved in the Climax MUST be the conflict engaged by the protagonist in the First Act Break. This is perhaps the only unbreakable rule in screenwriting.

- There are always exceptions, but generally speaking, once the movie is essentially over at the conclusion of the Climax, don't waste too much time in a lengthy Denouement. Your audience will be ready to exit the theater. Don't annoy them by demanding they remain for any longer than is necessary to tie a satisfying bow on the story.

- Three Act Structure isn't conformist behavior or the enemy of creativity. It is simply the most common method by which narrative drama is conveyed. If you strive for originality, doing so with your story as an atypical structure won't distinguish you in any way if your content is lacking. It will simply make weak or inferior writing more confusing and harder to follow.

WRITING EXERCISE:
BREAKING DOWN YOUR FAVORITES

The following exercise is designed to assist you in becoming more familiar with Three Act Structure, as well as the key plot points you've just learned about.

Pick five films you know extremely well, are willing to revisit, or are interested in seeing for the first time. They must have a traditional Three Act Structure. No *Pulp Fiction* or *Memento*, sorry. Next, identify the 7 Major Plot Points of each.

Don't forget that some of the answers will be individual scenes, while others may be sequences or a succession of scenes.

An example... *The Hangover*:

The Inciting Incident — Phil, Stu, and Alan wake up in their trashed hotel suite, memories gone, a tiger in the bathroom, a baby in the closet, and no sign of Doug.

The First Act Break — They search their pockets to discover clues about their forgotten night, then retrieve a stolen police car from the valet and leave the hotel to retrace their steps and find Doug.

An Early Complication — Stu apparently got married... to a stripper... and used Grandma's ring!

The Midpoint — Attacked by Mr. Chow and his goons, the guys are led to believe Doug is being held hostage and will only be released upon the return of Mr. Chow's 80 thousand dollars.

The Second Act Break — Having bought the wrong Doug, Phil finally surrenders and calls Tracy to explain they've misplaced the groom and won't make it back for the wedding.

The Climax — Speeding from Vegas to LA, the quartet changes en route and arrives late, but in time for the I do's.

The Denouement — The wedding reception, followed by the missing pictures from their forgotten night in Vegas.

CHAPTER 2

Genre...
Get to Know Your Audience

One of the more overlooked elements of screenwriting is the concept of audience identification. More often than not, screenwriters lacking in experience tend to ignore the expectations of the audience because their focus is squarely on the construction of the script itself: plot, story, characters, etc., all from their very narrow perspective. It is a common indicator of amateur work and a red flag for the industry you hope to seduce with your writing.

It may seem like an abstract consideration but it truly is not. What will the audience expect to see or feel? What will they want from the film? What might send them home happy or conversely, leave them hugely disappointed? If you don't know and/or don't consider who your audience is or will be, how can you expect to successfully write for them? To ignore the needs and expectations of your audience is to set yourself up for failure from the very beginning of the process. I think we can agree... that would be an awful lot of work for nothing.

It's one thing to know you are writing a comedy and another thing entirely to understand that not all comedies are built the same, appeal to the same audience, or deliver humor in the same ways. What makes some laugh, might very often offend others.

In much the same way, the expectations of your audience can dramatically change whether you make *The Shining* or *Saw*, *2001: A Space Odyssey* or *Spaceballs*, *The Goonies* or *National Treasure*. Is the audience for the *Twilight* franchise the same as for *Underworld?* Considering both place the battle between vampires and were-wolves front and center, one might expect it to be so, yet they are vastly different. Understanding the elements of audience identification impacts tone, pacing, dialogue, character, plot, and every other aspect of a script so it is best to pay attention to the needs of your intended demographic.

The obvious examples of this are things like cursing, nudity, and extreme violence. You won't see them in family pictures or anything geared towards children for obvious reasons. It gets more complicated understanding that audiences have certain expectations when they attend an action movie or a romantic comedy for example. Some movies appeal to a predominantly male audience, while others skew female. Age can play a role, as can education, political, and/or moral beliefs, religion, as well as many other factors.

The most important aspect of this to remember is that when you try and please too many people, you invariably end up pleasing no one. It's like a politician who tries to say what they think everyone wants to hear. The problem is that people want different things and you simply can't satisfy everybody. Movies are the same way. If you try and accommodate every audience, you won't appeal to any of them, teasing each with morsels, but none will get a full meal.

Understanding the attributes associated with each basic genre will provide you "compass bearings" with regards to style, tone, character, theme, and pacing, among other elements. Additionally, recognizing the basic ingredients of genre and audience identification will help you to avoid clichés and stereotypes. Finally, taking the time to consider the expectations of your audience is not only the best way to meet them, but also to see where you can defy and exceed them.

FAMILY FILMS

The only genre that regularly crosses all demographic lines is family films. The unique aspect of family films is that they are the only genre that is first and foremost about the audience. Though family films are a distinct genre unto themselves, in truth, they are actually a film from another genre, conceived and written to appeal to children and occasionally their parents as well.

That's why you have family pictures that are action, comedy, musical, drama, science fiction, and even horror. *Spy Kids, Home Alone, The Wizard of Oz, My Girl, Wall-E, and Monster House* being examples of each.

Exceptional family films have the broadest audience because they entertain children while also being palatable, or even enjoyable for their parents. Their innocence and lack of controversy allows them to generally cross both racial and gender lines, as well as socioeconomic, religious, and political divides.

There is a common industry term that represents these types of movies with mass audience appeal… **The Four Quadrant Film**. This is a marketing and industry term that you don't really need to pay much attention to, but for the purposes of understanding why family films are so appealing from a business perspective, this easily explains it. Quite simply, the four quadrants are young, old, male, and female. These are the four basic audiences that exist, without further being broken down by race, religion, or other factors.

Family films are the most common to be included in this rare classification. Successful films that fall into this category often earn iconic or classic status and are among some of the more cherished films of all time. Examples include *The Wizard of Oz, Cars, Toy Story, The Lion King, The Sound of Music*, and *The Christmas Story*.

Some of the common expectations from a family audience include:

- Political Correctness
- Nothing Overtly Offensive (e.g., Sex, Violence, Language)
- Humor
- Morality Issues
- Ethical Dilemmas
- Life Lessons
- Love of Family
- Friendship
- A Sense of Wonder & Awe
- Kids vs. Adults
- Children Saving the Day
- Fairy Tales
- Wish Fulfillment

Music and animation are also often associated with family films.

ACTION

While family films are first and foremost about the audience, action movies are all about tone, hence the name. Additionally, be aware that the #1 moviegoing audience is young males, which is why the summer months, when school is out, are filled with high-octane action films.

Action film fans expect adventure and excitement above all else. They may want the hero to get the girl (or guy as the case may be), but they buy their ticket to watch them save the day. Once again, remember that the varying expectations of your audience determine whether you are making *Bad Boys* or *Kill Bill*, *The Fast and the Furious* or *Taken*, *Mad Max* or *Dirty Harry*.

Of particular importance in the action genre is a dynamic villain or worthy opponent for your protagonist, making for a far more compelling audience experience. Don't lose sight of this as you will notice that the best action films tend to have great antagonists, and those that often fall flat do so because the fight is too one sided, and therefore boring and/or lacking in inspiration or excitement.

Some of the common expectations from an action audience include:

- Fast Pace
- Excitement
- Violence
- Good and Evil
- Heroism
- Clearly Defined Stakes
- BIG Set Pieces and Explosions

- People in Jeopardy
- Sex
- Gadgetry
- Masculinity and/or Machismo
- Dire Consequences for Failure
- Suspense and Tension
- <u>A Worthy Opponent</u>

COMEDY

As with action, comedy is the second major genre dictated primarily by tone. The obvious number one priority is humor, which above all other factors, is what draws people to a particular film from this genre. Your audience is there to laugh so you better make sure you bring the funny.

You must recognize that not all comedy is amusing to everyone. Once again, understanding your audience will help you cater to their expectations. There is satire, black comedy, physical, spoof, raunchy, sophisticated, etc.

Night at the Museum has a different audience than *American Pie*, which in turn has a different audience from *Bad Santa*, *The Naked Gun*, *Annie Hall*, *Trading Places*, *The Waterboy*, and Tyler Perry's *Madea* films. If you want to be successful in this genre, you absolutely must have an understanding of what is funny to your particular audience.

Some of the common expectations from a comedy audience include:

- Humor — obvious, but worth repeating!
- Fast Pace
- Happy Endings
- Outrageous Situations
- Odd and/or Quirky Characters
- Charming Leads
- Unusual or Unlikely Settings

HORROR

Along with action and comedy, the same rules apply to horror movies, the last of the three primary genres where tone is the top priority of your audience. They are there to be frightened so above all else, you better make sure to deliver on that core expectation!

Some horror films are awash in blood and gore. In these cases, the horror is often more visceral. They generally play to a younger crowd and rely heavily on surprise with a killer jumping out of the dark to terrify his or her intended victim(s) before they  get cut, hacked, sawed, or sliced. This subgenre of horror is sometimes referred to in the industry as torture porn. It includes such films as *Saw*, *Hostel*, and *The Texas Chainsaw Massacre*.

Other variations of horror can skew more sophisticated, relying on psychology, religion, and the occult to create, instill, or augment terror. Examples of this include *The Shining*, *The Exorcist*, *Rosemary's Baby*, and *The Others*.

In either case, the audience is there to be uncomfortable. Ideally, they don't know what's coming, only that it will be scary when it arrives. Death is generally the most typical consequence faced by each  character as horror is often about survival, either that of the main character or perhaps many more as well.

A final important point with regards to horror films is that quite often, the antagonist is the most prominent and important role in the script and story, as opposed to the protagonist. Can you name the lead in any of the *Friday the 13th* films? Does it matter? Freddy Krueger, Jigsaw, Chucky, et al. are the memorable characters from movies in this genre so you better have a truly electrifying villain if you're going to play in this particular sandbox. This isn't to say you should abandon efforts to craft an engaging protagonist, but often in horror, the unique qualities of the antagonist are more captivating than who's being pursued, slaughtered, haunted, or harassed.

Some of the common expectations from a horror audience include:

- Scary Situations
- Blood
- Death & Violence
- Psychological Problems
- Crazy Killers
- Serial Murder
- Rituals
- Religious Hysteria
- Demonic Possession
- DYNAMIC ANTAGONIST

ACTION, COMEDY, and HORROR films are primarily about **TONE**. The audience is there to be excited, scared, or humored, and ideally for it to be done in a manner that is fresh and new.

The word formulaic isn't necessarily bad or something to be feared. Be creative and always aim for originality, but don't be timid about treading on familiar territory. The goal within these genres isn't to reinvent the wheel, it's to use your creativity to take an existing wheel and give it a bold, new look.

You think the writers of the Jason Bourne trilogy are unaware of a certain British secret agent? How about the numerous films, both good and bad, that can be described as *Die Hard* in a bus, plane, space station, submarine, shopping mall, etc., etc., etc.

How many vampire movies can you think of? Can you explain the difference between Jason Voorhees and Leatherface? You think the creators of *Superbad* and *American Pie* never saw *Porky's*?

The bottom line is while I know the white hat will almost always defeat the black hat, the guy and girl will usually wind up together, and a film in one of these genres is likely to have a happy ending, the trick isn't to avoid this, but to figure out a way to get there in a fresh, inventive, and entertaining manner.

THE SNOOZE BAR

The Snooze Bar is a simple device I created to help screenwriters and specifically those working in the action, comedy, and horror genres, as well as any subgenres such as thriller, adventure, or mystery where tone is also the principal audience expectation. It is incumbent upon you as the screenwriter to consistently deliver those tonal beats in a timely fashion. The Snooze Bar assists in making that happen. Specifically, there should be no more than 10–12 pages between action, comedy, horror, or other genre specific elements in your script.

Though this may sound simplistic, consider how you would feel sitting in a movie theater, watching a comedy, and 10 to 12 minutes pass without any laughter. What about an action film and 10 minutes go by with nothing exciting happening? How entertained would you be?

Quite simply, from the outlining phase through to your final draft, be aware of long patches where you are failing to deliver on the primary expectation of your audience. Count the page gaps and determine if adjustments are needed. This isn't conforming or pandering; it isn't selling out to provide sufficient thrills in an action movie. Your mission is to make the action fresh, not to try and sell the notion that the absence of it somehow enhances your work.

SCIENCE FICTION & FANTASY

Science fiction & fantasy is distinctive in that it is primarily about the setting. Just as family films take from another genre and alter the film to suit a particular audience, sci-fi/fantasy does the same thing, but the setting becomes the focus.

The key to this genre is the mythology. Great sci-fi/fantasy boasts an engrossing, often elabo-rate mythology, the most successful of which often spawn far more than one picture because when you create an entire world, universe, or culture, there are always many additional stories that can be told.

Such is the case with *Star Wars*, *Star Trek*, *Harry Potter*, *Terminator*, *Stargate*, or more recently, *Avatar*. Appealing to this audience is all about detail... and a lot of it! You are creating a new world that includes a belief system, a moral code, religion, laws, rules to live by — and don't forget, the tools and tidbits of daily life. Money, food, weapons, trans-portation, etc.... It might even require a new language. Can you speak Klingon? How about Na'vi?

The reason films like *Excalibur* and *Clash of the Titans* are associ-ated with this genre is because they are similarly rooted in mythology. The mythologies of Arthurian England and the gods of Olympus may not have been recently conceived on a laptop, but rest assured, the intri-cate details of the worlds they embody are equally distinctive and as has been proven, extremely cinematic.

Most comic books also fall under this umbrella, typically in addi-tion to action. The term origin story is often applied to such films because they too establish a mythology. How Kal-El was transported from Krypton and grows up to become Superman. The death of Bruce Wayne's parents. Peter Parker being bitten by a mutant spider and his role in the death of his uncle. Not to mention the mortal enemies each has, as well as true loves and in the case of Superman, an Achilles heel in the form of Kryptonite.

They have iconic vehicles such as the Batmobile, draw power from unique sources such as Green Lantern's ring and use specific weaponry such as Captain America's shield, Thor's hammer, or Wonder Woman's lasso.

Success in sci-fi/fantasy resides in the level of detail you are able to deliver. Whether it's the creation of arguably the greatest prop ever: the lightsaber, the fact that Superman draws his power from Earth's yellow sun, or a guiding mythology, such as the "Gathering" in the *Highlander* franchise, these nuances help to facilitate the successful creation of truly imaginary worlds. Just take a look at *Harry Potter* and realize how complex and detailed those stories are with Quidditch, Muggles, and Butterbeer as examples. Consider the possibilities created with this very familiar line...

"A Long Time Ago In a Galaxy Far, Far Away..."

The only limit is your imagination.

Some of the common expectations from a sci-fi/fantasy audience include:

- A Detailed Mythology
- Adventure
- A World of True Imagination
- Captivating Visuals
- Alternate Realities
- Manipulation of History
- Time Travel
- Life and Death Stakes
- A Dynamic Villain
- Unique Technology, Gadgetry, and/or Weaponry
- Heroism

A final note with regards to science fiction & fantasy is that the audience is largely masculine... not male, though it is, but masculine. Even in the case of the *Alien* franchise, which boasts a female protagonist, the audience skews male. This is highlighted because again, you MUST consider who your audience is. For most films in this genre, the action and adventure are generally more vital to the overall success than the love story or other elements.

In the case of *Harry Potter*, it becomes a marriage of family and fantasy as both the setting and wide appeal to children are equally prioritized. The expectations of both genres are successfully employed to reach a broader audience.

In other instances, the emphasis on romance over action can tip the scale towards a more feminine audience. Such is the case with the *Twilight* or *Hunger Games* franchises. The trend towards romance is also why women comprise the bulk of the audiences for both *The Vampire Diaries* and *True Blood*.

This is also why female-driven action is so rare. Can you name a successful sci-fi/fantasy franchise, other than the aforementioned *Alien*, driven by a female lead? *Tomb Raider* might have worked, but the execution was poor. This is also one of the main reasons why we've seen multiple *Iron Man*, *Superman*, and *X-Men* films, but Warner Brothers has struggled to crack *Wonder Woman*. While *Batman* has been rebooted several times, a new *Catwoman* film isn't likely to hit theaters anytime soon. *Wolverine* has multiple standalone films, as does *Iron Man*, but you're far less likely to see movies based on *Storm* or *Black Widow*.

The Hunger Games is likely the most successful which shows that rare doesn't mean impossible and in fact, Hollywood is smartly beginning to realize that female-driven franchises can be hugely successful when executed well. That's really the key because for every *Hunger Games* or *Divergent*, there's also a *Mortal Instruments* or *Vampire Academy*.

WESTERN

Westerns are simply worth noting because like science fiction and fantasy, they are also about setting for the simple reason that they employ a significant and extremely rich mythology. Westerns rely on established elements such as cowboys, gunfights, saloons, unique clothing, and especially horses, as well as the presence of the American Indian, among many other details.

In much the same way that family films alter audience expectations to shift between comedy, drama, action, and fantasy, westerns similarly can affect different tones while always maintaining the mythology and thereby the setting. The presence of comedy delivers a film like *Blazing Saddles* or *The Three Amigos*; action brings you

Tombstone or *Young Guns*; drama delivers a film like *Unforgiven*; and even science fiction occurs such as in *Westworld* or *Cowboys vs. Aliens*.

Just as many science-fiction or fantasy mythologies are revisited time and again, such as with vampires, Robin Hood, Camelot, or ancient Greece, westerns have many that are employed time and again as well. The Lone Ranger, Zorro, Billy the Kid, Wyatt Earp, and Jesse James all being examples.

DRAMA

What sets drama apart is its emphasis on character and the interpersonal relationships between individuals. Drama is typically more about who than what. Identify the "who" and you immediately have a much clearer sense of the audience and their expectations.

Are you making a movie about high school romance, the bonds of soldiers in combat, coming out of the closet in your 40s, dying from cancer, infidelity, etc.?

Take infidelity as an example. Extending it a step further, are the expectations the same for a film like *Unfaithful* as they are for a film like *Soul Food*? What about *Terms of Endearment*, *My Girl*, and *The Bucket List*? All three films deal with death, but for different audiences and from entirely different perspectives.

Drama is personal. Successful drama touches people. It speaks to them, which above all else, means it must be relatable to your audience. How do you achieve that? Your best option is to create situations that strike to the core of one or more groups of people, such as the temptation to stray from your marriage, the prognosis of death, alcoholism, divorce, the death of a child, etc.

Alternatively, not everyone can relate to what it feels like to be in combat, but if you can relate to the character that is experiencing it, you are far more likely to make an emotional connection with your audience; therefore, a second or complimentary option is to create characters that the audience can identify with.

The #1 priority of ANY and ALL screenwriters is to make the audience care about the characters in their story, regardless of genre. It is what holds their interest above and beyond anything else. Imagine how much greater importance this takes on if you are working in the one genre that is defined by its emphasis on character. It is for this reason above all others that flaws are most evident in dramatic screenplays. Explosions and humor can camouflage certain literary missteps, but in drama, there's simply no place for weak writing to hide.

You must strive to create emotional connections between the audience and your characters. Perhaps the audience will sympathize with the cancer struggle in *Terms of Endearment* or maybe they take pride in the selflessness of Oskar Schindler. They could understand the addiction that plagues Nicolas Cage in *Leaving Las Vegas* or are similarly angered by racial injustice, as in *Crash*.

Some of the common expectations from a drama audience include:

- Serious Tone
- Authentic Characters
- Real Life
- Relatable Conflicts
- Familiar Dilemmas
- Life Altering Stakes
- Passion For Something
- True Stories
- A Cause Worth Fighting For
- Complex Relationships
- A Significant Internal Struggle
- Ethical and/or Moral Questions
- Character Growth or Change
- Deep Emotional Struggles

ROMANTIC COMEDY

One additional genre worth mentioning here is romantic comedy. Don't let the word comedy in the label fool you. A traditional romantic comedy is not actually a comedy. You aren't supposed to laugh out loud throughout the movie. The emphasis is on the romance, which is why it gets top billing. It's a fun, breezy love story. The audience is supposed to smile, occasionally laugh, but above all else, be charmed by the couple at the heart of the story.

The ultimate example is *Pretty Woman*. There are some funny bits, but mostly it's sweet and charming. Is Meg Ryan's fake orgasm in *When Harry Met Sally* laugh-out-loud funny? Of course it is, but more so because it's a rare moment that stands out. Films like *The Proposal*, *How to Lose a Guy in 10 Days*, *You've Got Mail*, and *The Philadelphia Story* are not comedies, so don't kill yourself trying to come up with punch lines when emulating their formula. Looking at the Snooze Bar, your goal is consistent relationship moments, not comedic beats.

Recognize that the expectations of your audience are to smile while they enjoy watching a couple fall in love. A perfect example of this being ignored is the poorly received *The Break-Up*. Making an audience smile while watching a couple fall in hate with each other is quite an undertaking and it should come as no surprise that the attempt failed. Had the attempt been made as part of a true comedy and not as a backwards try at a reverse romantic comedy, it likely would have been more successful.

Some might argue against this assertion, citing a film like *The 40-Year-Old Virgin* as a prime example of a laugh-out-loud romantic comedy. However, it isn't a romantic comedy — it is a straight comedy that has a relationship as a major subplot. It may seem like a small, even semantic difference, but it's important to recognize why it's not. The love story is NOT the primary conflict or focus of the film. *The 40-Year-Old Virgin* is about Steve Carell losing his virginity and the reasons why it hasn't happened yet. His relationship with Catherine Keener is in support of that plot.

The lesson here is that despite the label, the primary audience expectation for a romantic comedy is the relationship, not humor. The presence of comedy can be a nice bonus, but it should not be your primary objective when working in this genre. If you don't believe me, do a Google search for the top romantic comedies and gauge for yourself how many are hilarious or just charming.

EVERY GENRE, from the ones listed to others such as disaster, slapstick, sports, mystery, thriller, adventure, and so on, have their own set of expectations. Take the time to consider what they are. Understand who your audience is. Doing so will allow you to not only give them what they want, but to also push the boundaries and defy their expectations where it makes sense to do so.

This is an extremely important point because I am not trying to put everyone in nice, tidy little compartments or force everyone to apply some mathematic formula to screenwriting. It is always encouraged that you, as a screenwriter, be creative and deliver unexpected surprises. This isn't possible, however, if you don't consider what's expected to begin with it.

It is this skill that also allows a screenwriter to reposition or repurpose an established story for a different audience, often transitioning to a completely different genre in the process. Examples of this include

The Seven Samurai becoming *The Magnificent Seven*; *Emma* to *Clueless*; *Pygmalion* to *She's All That* or even *Trading Places*; *The Odyssey* to *O Brother, Where Art Thou?*; *Dangerous Liaisons* to *Cruel Intentions*; and *A Christmas Carol* being the inspiration for countless films like *Scrooged*, *Ghosts of Girlfriends Past*, or *The Muppet Christmas Carol* among hordes of other adaptations.

I believe we can agree that the audience for *Pygmalion* or *My Fair Lady* and that of *She's All That* and *Trading Places* are decidedly different. Making such a transition is only possible if the screenwriter is aware of the new set of expectations held by the targeted audience. It's also how you can take a Heist movie and make it a spoof, an adventure, or even science fiction. *Love at First Bite, Twilight, 30 Days of Night, Underworld,* and *Dracula* may all deal with vampire lore and mythology, but the audiences for these films are completely different and the ability to recognize how to appeal to each will substantially help your efforts to be a successful screenwriter.

KEYS TO REMEMBER

- Professional screenwriters know whom they are writing for. They know who the audience for the movie will be, and therefore are more able to meet their expectations as they actually consider them throughout the writing process.
- Family films are about the audience. They are films from other genres written and conceived for a youthful demographic so above and beyond anything else, make sure they speak kid and don't offend Mom or Dad.
- Action, comedy, and horror are first and foremost about tone. Delivering on the core expectation of these audiences is your primary mission. It is stunning how many screenwriters miss this oh so obvious point and submit boring action, comedy without laughter, and horror minus any thrills or chills.

- Particularly in action and horror, as well as their subgenres, the inclusion of a dynamic and memorable villain or antagonist is a prerequisite for success.
- In films driven by tone, you will commonly have a formulaic story. This is NOT to be feared, but rather embraced as a challenge. No one doubts James Bond or the Avengers will defeat the bad guys or that there will be at least one survivor of the Nightmare on Elm Street, but if you are creative in reaching such conclusions, people won't mind the predictability that often exists.
- Monitoring the consistent delivery of core expectations is both simple and necessary to the success of any screenplay, especially those driven by tone.
- Science fiction and fantasy are primarily about the setting and must include a rich and engaging mythology. Success in this genre is 100% about the details.
- Drama is driven by character and interpersonal relationships. Successful drama typically has a distinct point of view about a specific issue or dilemma and connects on an emotional level with the intended audience, often by dealing with relatable subject matter.
- Mistakes and poor writing are most obvious in drama. Other genres have devices such as humor or explosions that can camouflage certain flaws, but drama has no such protection, which is why it is the most difficult genre to write exceptionally well.

WRITING EXERCISE: Genre Bending

This is an effective writing exercise that not only incorporates the lessons of genre and audience identification, but also those of dialogue and character, among others.

You will take a basic set up and write 3 scenes of no more than 3–5 pages.

Some possible setups:
1. Job interview
2. Father explaining sex to his child
3. Wife or husband shares a secret with their spouse
4. Passenger tries to cheer up a cab driver
5. Teenage boy hits on his friend's mother or vice versa
6. A marriage proposal
7. A lawyer questions a witness in court
8. A fight over a parking space
9. A driver talks to a cop after being pulled over
10. A doctor explains a diagnosis to his or her patient

Take the last one, the doctor and his or her patient. Now write three versions, one comedy, one urban drama, and one family. Imagine the possibilities. In the comedy, the diagnosis could be for excessive sweating or foot odor while the urban drama might be the need for a costly bone marrow transplant that insurance won't cover. You get the picture.

What about the fight over a parking space? Write one thriller version, one action, and one science fiction. Three very different scenes — are there parking spaces on the moon? There can be if you are the writer!

What about number 5? That could be humorous such as in *American Pie* or the dramatic precursor to a rape that rips a community apart.

This exercise simply gets you thinking about possibilities and that's an important key to effective screenwriting. Experiment. See what works. Try different approaches. Consider alternatives and new ideas.

CHAPTER 3

Character...

Indifference Is the Enemy

M*aking the audience care about your characters is your #1 PRIORITY!*

Fail to accomplish this and your script won't be worth the paper it's printed on. Even if the emotion is a negative one such as hatred or anger, that's not a problem as indifference is your true enemy. Indifference to your characters means the audience has no investment in their journey, and therefore no interest in whatever story you are telling. Conversely, you can make a film about paint drying and people will happily watch it if they genuinely care why the characters find that activity fascinating, inspiring, or whatever the case may be.

An example of this is how many excellent sports movies have been made about sports many people couldn't care less about. How many *Rocky* fans are actually boxing fans? How many people that enjoyed *Seabiscuit* have ever even been to a horse race? Do you need to love baseball to enjoy *Bull Durham*?

Another is sequels, which are so popular because they cater to an existing audience desiring to spend more time with characters they've already become familiar with. Look at the failures *Speed 2* and *US Marshals*. People wanted to see Keanu Reeves and Sandra Bullock in a different adventure, not her trapped in another runaway vehicle with Jason Patric as her replacement SWAT boyfriend. In the latter example, they wanted Tommy Lee Jones' US Marshal to go after another fugitive, but not another innocent one! That's a bad remake... not a sequel.

Generally speaking, it should be a writer's intention to have an audience like, fear, admire, despise, sympathize, and/or support the actions of most characters, particularly the protagonist. Character empathy is vitally important, but how is it achieved?

There are 4 basic truths of human nature:
1. We care about characters we feel sorry for.
2. We care about characters that possess traits we admire.
3. We care about people who practice charity and compassion for others.
4. We care about people we are physically attracted to.

The first three are self-explanatory and the reasons why are evident. In the case of the last one, don't fear the superficial or taboo. Ideally, make it work to your advantage. Embrace what real people can relate to. In the classic fairy tale *Beauty and the Beast*, people's obsession with one's physical appearance is at the heart of the story, as is the lesson learned by the Beast who must ultimately see past all of that to realize that he is more than his frightful appearance.

Many screenplays also include characters intended to strike fear or elicit negative feelings in an audience. The antagonist, particularly in proactive genres such as action, is the most obvious of these. Therefore, characters lacking the above traits can effectively generate the desired negative emotions from an audience. Remember, indifference is your enemy, not hate, loathing, or fear, which are simply the flip sides of the positive emotions you will look to generate for the other characters in your story.

The most compelling and potent of characters will often possess a combination of both the positive and negative. It is in these cases that characters feel genuine and most like real people who are never all good or all bad. For example, flawed heroes, villains with clouded or conflicting motivations, or common individuals who act in surprising and unpredictable ways such as John McClane, Gordon Gekko, or Ben Braddock.

Beyond making a character sympathetic or charismatic, an additional means by which audience identification can be achieved is to put the character in jeopardy. If a character's life is in danger, the audience will be at least marginally invested in whether they survive. Similarly, heroism is always attractive. A character that places someone else's safety above their own and risks danger to aid another will always engender positive feelings.

Humor is another powerful weapon in your arsenal. Genre and audience expectations are important elements to consider when including humor or comedy in your screenplay, but there is perhaps no better method to make an audience embrace a character than to make them funny.

In general, you want to create characters that people either want to be, want to be with, or absolutely can't be around out of fear, intolerance, disgust, or some other powerfully negative emotion. In terms of villains and antagonists, make them a worthy opponent because anything less and victory will seem predictable and bittersweet!

Great characters also routinely contradict themselves in terms of their actions not necessarily tracking with their personalities. As an example, look at Jack Nicholson in *As Good As It Gets*. He's rude, abrasive, and generally unappealing, yet the audience is allowed to see the warmth and vulnerability in his heart as he pursues a relationship with Helen Hunt and befriends Greg Kinnear.

Real people, even the good ones, often can't get out of their own way. They're attracted to individuals who are no good for them, embrace dangerous activities that could have dire consequences, abuse substances, and time and again make bad decisions, often knowing precisely how stupid, reckless, or naïve they are being. Incorporating this level of nuance and authenticity in your characters is one of the qualities that separate amateur writing from that of a professional.

INTERNAL AND EXTERNAL STRUGGLE

Most, if not all great characters, face both an internal and external conflict. In most cases, they successfully deal with both, arriving at what many call a Hollywood or happy ending. In other instances, where appropriate, a character fails to resolve a conflict resulting in tragic or unforeseen conclusions. In either case, the internal and external struggles should both exist.

The External Struggle is often the core conflict of the movie. Saving the planet from impending doom, solving a crime, catching a killer, winning the heart of one's true love, ending a curse, etc.

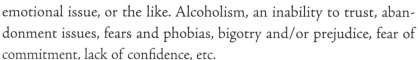

The Internal Struggle tends to be a complication resulting from a character flaw, personality quirk, emotional issue, or the like. Alcoholism, an inability to trust, abandonment issues, fears and phobias, bigotry and/or prejudice, fear of commitment, lack of confidence, etc.

It is entirely possible, if not probable, that a character may face more than one of each of these struggles. It is also quite possible for the internal struggle to be the core conflict. In fact, that is quite common in dramas where character is the defining element. Perhaps getting sober is the plot of your film or maybe it's a protagonist

getting past his/her own racism leading to the acceptance of another character in their lives.

DRAMATIC NEED

What does your character want? What does he or she seek? What is he or she trying to achieve? What are his or her goals?

In order for a goal to function well, it must include 3 critical elements:

1. **Stakes** — What happens if the goal is not met or achieved? What is the cost? What will be lost or sacrificed?

2. **Opposition** — Someone or something formidable must stand in the way of meeting or achieving the goal.

3. **Challenge** — Meeting and/or achieving the goal should require hard work, ingenuity, and perseverance in the face of opposition. Any goal realized with minimal effort won't be satisfying to your audience.

CHANGE

How will characters change during the course of your film, particularly your protagonist? How will facing the conflict(s) of your story alter their personality or any other element of their psychology? This is critical because a character that is unchanged by whatever journey you take them on will feel one note and generic. This transition from beginning to end is often referred to as a character arc, a term you have likely heard before.

If people are, as most believe, the sum of their experiences, your characters can be no different; since the experience they endure in your film will likely be the most dynamic of their lives, profound change is both expected AND required. If, in looking at your outline or script, they remain static or unchanged from beginning to end, carefully consider

how you might adjust that. If you don't, the script will greatly suffer and it will stand out as a negative to any industry reader.

If it is an action film and they must save the world, can you really expect them not to feel the pressure of those stakes or to worry about the consequences of failure? How about a horror movie? Your protagonist goes into the woods with her closest friends and fiancé and one by one, they are each picked off, leaving her as the sole survivor. Would you expect her to be unchanged by such an ordeal? These are extreme scenarios, but no more so than a character falling in love, overcoming a disease, facing a loved one's mortality, or any other significant life experience. Your characters must evolve in a manner that reflects the events faced during the time period of your story and screenplay.

CAN WE RELATE?

Successfully drawn characters often feel familiar to an audience because they've personally faced similar issues. It might be men relating to Michael Douglas' struggle with fidelity in *Fatal Attraction*. It could also be a young girl's dreams of being a princess such as in *The Princess Diaries* or the visceral fear of sharks in *Jaws*. How about the question of whether men and women can be friends, the main theme of *When Harry Met Sally?*

Capture the zeitgeist! That was one of the reasons *Up in the Air* was so successful. It came at a time when people could relate to losing a job and facing unemployment.

Tap into primal urges and fears. *Arachnophobia* is the title of a movie for a reason. *Taken* is a good example of a film exploiting a parent's fears of their child being abducted and placed in imminent danger. The  more people can relate to your story, the more successful you will be.

CONFLICT IS INTERESTING!

Don't be afraid of taboos, political incorrectness, prejudices, or the like. Look at the film *In the Heat of the Night*. The black character of Detective Virgil Tibbs is obviously going to face tremendous racism and bigotry in the deep south of 1960s Mississippi. For that reason, it wasn't necessary to make Rod Steiger's Chief Gillespie racist, but doing so, despite his being a relatively good guy and making the friction between Steiger and Sidney Poitier integral to the story, elevates the film from a run of the mill police procedural  to an iconic and classic film worth your time and admiration.

Since you are also working hard to create characters worthy of an actor's best efforts, the more complex the character, the more appealing the role becomes. Opposites attract. Allies don't always agree and sibling rivalry can range from liking the same boy at school all the way to fratricide. Don't allow everyone to just get along. Even amongst friends, dysfunction makes for more compelling drama than the blandness of easy camaraderie and friendly cooperation.

THE ANTAGONIST

Great villains are often more engaging than the heroes that vanquish them. One of the most common mistakes in screenwriting is ignoring the antagonist, relegating them to a stock figure that briefly appears at the beginning and end of a story. Aside from this being a wasted opportunity, bear in mind the point that's been made several times already which is that victory that comes with little or no challenge will never be satisfying to an audience. A worthy opponent is far more compelling. Additionally, their shady intentions, twisted motives, and ability to do what decent people, including your protagonist, won't, make them fun to create and write.

Why are they bad, evil, misguided, obstructive, destructive, or just generally in the way? What are their motives? Finally, what, beyond simply raising the body count or adding more blood can elevate their duplicity, villainy, or relative sliminess? I would caution that adding more dead bodies rarely accomplishes much. In fact, it can work against you in that it almost numbs the audience to the violence. What is more visceral, one painful and tragic death of a familiar character or a hundred faceless victims?

Cruelty to animals is another very compelling option. It may not make much sense, but an audience would much prefer your villain stab another person through the heart than kick a cute puppy. What do

you think would unsettle an audience more, an antagonist beating up another character with a baseball bat or quietly sitting in a chair, ripping the wings off a fluttering butterfly?

SUPPORTING ROLES

First and foremost, make sure they advance the story in some way; otherwise, why are they present in your screenplay?

A supporting character often has the ability to steal scenes. They don't necessarily need to possess the same qualities of the protagonist, which should be looked upon as a valuable opportunity, not to be squandered. There is far more freedom to make them quirky, funny, scary, or outrageous in a way that wouldn't work for the main character, but breathes life into your script and story.

While it's important to make all your characters pop, you have limited time to develop them and you don't want your focus — or that of your audience — to become distracted. As such, I am a MAJOR advocate of choosing one supporting character in particular to make really special. Whether you make them distractingly funny, duplicitous, smarmy, slutty, or anything else that captures the attention of the audience, a truly memorable supporting role often has the potential to make a good movie great. Certainly, the actor's performance contributes substantially to this, but much of it must already exist on the page, long before the casting process begins.

Would anyone really remember *My Cousin Vinny* without Mona Lisa Vito? How about Curly in *City Slickers* or Captain Renault from *Casablanca*? What about Duckie in *Pretty in Pink*? Consider a film like *Father of the Bride*. Martin Short made Franck Eggelhoffer memorable, but where that character could have been just a run-of-the-mill wedding planner, instead, he was anything but. His many idiosyncrasies became one of the film's greatest assets and sources of comedy. One of the most intriguing supporting characters of all time, and perhaps more so because he had no dialogue, is Chewbacca. Consider the choices made with that character. They weren't obvious, but it would be hard to argue against the genius that is Chewy.

Supporting characters can also fill an emotional void such as Ralph Bellamy's Mr. Morris in *Pretty Woman*. Richard Gere's lifelong obsession with his father makes him ruthless. This aggression is so ingrained, it has bled into his personal life, making intimacy a challenge. In the end, doing right by Morris becomes tantamount to earning the pride and respect of his own father, the result being Edward is psychologically cured and able to love freely, much to the delight of Julia Roberts and Darryl the chauffeur.

In the earliest stages of your script's development, identify which of your supporting characters has the potential to affect your story as substantially as those mentioned above. If none do, create one. In either case, use your creativity to deliver a fresh and distinctive supporting role that will stand out from all the rest and thereby add tremendous value to your work.

TOO MANY CHARACTERS VS. ENSEMBLES

Take care to limit the number of characters you have to what's absolutely necessary to achieve success with your script and story. Too many characters can create a myriad of problems such as:

1. Audience/reader confusion
2. Unnecessary length... more setup requires more resolution
3. You spread the story too thin
4. Characters with overlapping purposes
5. Too much dialogue

Scripts boasting large ensemble casts are no exception and require special handling. Sports movies, jury pictures, and war films all necessitate large casts, but not all characters are created equally.

George Clooney is the obvious lead in *Ocean's 11*. Whether facing off with antagonist Andy Garcia, plotting with sidekick Brad Pitt, sparring with love interest Julia Roberts, or recruiting protégé Matt Damon, it's Clooney's Danny Ocean who drives the story. Even with an ensemble, you will have 1 or 2 roles who get substantial storylines and it simply radiates out from there, with everyone else receiving less and less attention.

GEORGE CLOONEY
Brad Pitt & Julia Roberts
Matt Damon & Andy Garcia
Don Cheadle, Elliott Gould & Bernie Mac
Scott Caan, Casey Affleck & Carl Reiner
hacker & contortionist

The clearest names above are the leads and key supporting players in *Ocean's 11* with the most significant backstories, subplots, and agendas. As you can see, each level down the names get smaller, just as the amount of attention paid to the characters diminishes as well. The bottom two are labeled hacker and contortionist because most people remember them by their function more so than their names, which further illustrates the point.

Similarly, while we may spend time with John Cassavetes, Jim Brown, and Telly Savalas in *The Dirty Dozen*, the primary focus is on Lee Marvin and Charles Bronson. There will always be exceptions to the rules provided, but the best way to bend or break the rules is to learn and master them first.

In the case of *The Breakfast Club*, you have perhaps the truest ensemble movie ever: 5 kids, all sharing the role of protagonist and none more important than the others. One reason John Hughes could make that work is the near total absence of other characters in the film. He rarely left the kids. Paul Gleason embodied a memorable foil and the only other character in the film is the sly Janitor… look at that, a minor but memorable supporting character adding substantial value to a great script.

ROLE REVERSAL

This refers to situations when the protagonist and antagonist effectively switch places in the sense that the protagonist is the "bad" guy and the antagonist is the white hat. It's uncommon, but presents some interesting dynamics to explore.

It is common in this circumstance for the so-called accused or outlaw to be framed or wrongly convicted with the audience aware of their innocence. This allows them to root for their exoneration. *The Fugitive* is an example of this. Harrison Ford is convicted of killing his wife and when his prison bus crashes, he escapes and sets off to prove his innocence. Meanwhile, the antagonist is Tommy Lee Jones' US Marshal who is moving heaven and Earth to capture him. Ford is the alleged criminal while Jones is the cop, but their roles are reversed.

It doesn't have to be a case of an innocent being wrongly accused or convicted, however. In *Out of Sight*, George Clooney is an escaped bank robber and thief. Jennifer Lopez is the US Marshal trying to bring him to justice. In this instance, your protagonist is an anti-hero, something that will be discussed later in this chapter.

When Your Antagonist Isn't a Person

The antagonist isn't always a person, but typical of these cases are extremely high stakes and a high concept that involves at least the protagonist's survival, if not many others as well. Examples include the asteroid in *Armageddon*, death in *The Bucket List* or *Love Story*, the apocalypse in *2012*, the island and isolation in *Castaway*, and the failing spacecraft in *Apollo 13*.

Dual Antagonists

There are a couple of scenarios that involve dual or multiple antagonists. The first is somewhat rarer and involves one antagonist being a person, while the other is an event or circumstance—such as Billy Zane and sinking in *Titanic*.

The other, far more common use of dual antagonists is typical of comic book or action films. In such cases, two or more major villains exist. Take note that this does not include a situation where a singular villain such as Darth Vader is lumped in with all the stormtroopers. Rather, this would be the Joker and Harvey "Two-Face" Dent in *The Dark Knight* or Jaws and Stromberg in *The Spy Who Loved Me*. This is frequently employed in such films because multiple heroes exist as well and they all need someone to battle in the Climax. While Captain America faces off with The Winter Soldier, Nick Fury and Black Widow must deal with Redford's Alexander Pierce, the revealed head of Hydra.

Just be mindful that when you use more than one antagonist, you MUST make sure each of the characters are sufficiently developed and afforded enough screen time to make them worthy as an opponent.

THE SAME CHARACTER

Occasionally, the protagonist and antagonist can be the same character. Often, this occurs when the protagonist is his or her own worst enemy. A character flaw or illness creates the core conflict that must be resolved. *Groundhog Day*, *As Good As It Gets*, and *Psycho* are examples of this.

Generally, in these cases, the core conflict involves conquering the internal struggle that makes the protagonist also the antagonist. As such, victory in the Climax often means the elimination of the antagonist in a fashion.

For example, in the many iterations of *A Christmas Carol*, Ebenezer Scrooge is shown glimpses of his life by the ghosts of past, present, and future. In so doing, he learns the meaning of charity, fellowship, and good will, thus removing the stain upon his soul and leaving only the reborn gentleman, warm, and caring, in the end.

ANTI-HEROES

They are successfully drawn when their fight is somehow sympathetic to an audience and/or they have a charm or sex appeal that transcends their misdeeds. Perhaps it is revenge as in the case of *The Punisher*, whose family was murdered, turning him into a vigilante. Maybe it's John Dillinger in *Public Enemies*, stealing from a corrupt system during the Great Depression. There's also Robin Hood, stealing from the rich to give to the poor.

In the case of mobster and gangster films, such as *The Godfather*, Michael Corleone operates from a code based on family and loyalty. It also helps that, in general, those he kills are criminals themselves and often worse than him. Pacino also gave us Tony Montana in *Scarface*. Beyond simply being a fascinating character, the audience is first made to sympathize with Tony's initial poverty and his struggle to make it in America, his desire to take care of his family, and his friendship with Manny. It's also fun to watch his empire take form.

Beatrix Kiddo in *Kill Bill* seeks revenge against a collection of assassins who attempted to kill her and killed her baby, or so she believes until B.B. turns out to be alive. In the underappreciated *Out of Sight*, George Clooney plays a career criminal, but he's charming, charismatic, and the audience is 100% rooting for him to escape in the end because they know he's harmless to others and even heroic, having saved Nancy Allen's character from being raped. It also shouldn't go without saying that his crimes were nonviolent bank robberies where nobody ever got hurt, a key to gaining the audience's sympathy and support.

A typical component of anti-hero films is that the fight or conflict is with an individual or group that is worse than the protagonist or their motives somehow possess a certain nobility or moral justification. *Dexter* is an example from television, but as a serial killer, could the audience support him if his victims were innocent? His appeal is sparked by the fact he only kills violent criminals who have gotten away with their own crimes as a result of a flawed judicial system. The audience not only can support this, but for many, it taps into a primal sense of justice rightly being served. He also has friends, a sister he loves (as only he can), and children that he cherishes.

Anti-Heroes are popular because they feel real. They possess flaws. They aren't square jawed, chiseled bits of perfection fighting for truth, justice, and the American way. Their motives may be a bit cloudy, as are their personalities, but the presence of control, compassion, or perhaps simply a moral code gives an audience permission to like and root for them.

CHARACTER BIOS

The more you get to know your characters, even their issues that may never come up in your story, the more they feel like real people and leap off the page.

Bios are an ideal way to quickly and easily develop your characters. Though it isn't necessary to do them for each, I heartily recommend you do so for at least your 3–5 primary roles. It need not take very long and there is no need to worry about formatting or appearance. Just start asking questions and write down words, phrases, fragments… bits and pieces that together form a distinct personality. There are no right or wrong answers.

Some of the things you come up with may find their way into the script. Others may not, but that's okay. Bios will also help you tremendously with regards to dialogue and distinct voice, a topic covered later in this text.

A few of the many questions to consider:

- Are they cynical?
- Do they vote?
- Are they an optimist or a pessimist?
- Conservative or liberal?
- Are they religious or spiritual?
- Are they moral or ethical?
- Are they a vegetarian and if so, why?
- Are they athletic or clumsy?
- Are they attractive? Vain?
- How do they view sex?
- Are they prejudiced and if so, are they aware of it?
- Is he a gentleman?
- Biggest pet peeve?
- Have they ever been in love?
- Do they keep secrets?
- Do they hold grudges?
- Do they have any medical issues?
- Does he have bad breath or does she smell like Doritos?
- Are they educated?
- Do things come easily to them?
- Have they ever had their heart broken?
- Have they ever faced death?
- Do they have children? Do they want them?
- Have they traveled? Are they cultured?

- Does she have good taste in clothing?
- Do they have any addictions?
- Where did they grow up?
- What's the worst thing they ever did as a child?

- Do they speak other languages?
- Were they abused as children?
- Are their parents alive?
- Do they obey 3 AM traffic lights?
- What's their greatest fear?
- Do they have siblings?

Let's assume you are doing a bio on a female protagonist in a comedy. You begin with standard biographical data such as birthplace, age, appearance, and so on. Now let's skip ahead to some more nuanced details. Taking a question from the list, does she have good taste in clothing? Let's say the answer is that she thinks she does, but in truth, she's utterly clueless and wears way too much pink. Is it safe to assume that such a simple fact to conceive would make it into the script? Is it likely that there will be a scene where her devotion to pink becomes fodder for some type of comedy? There you go; you've not only crafted a distinctive bit of personality, but you've also managed to give yourself an idea for a scene in the script.

How about a personal question that isn't on the list. Who is the most frustrating person in her life? I'm thinking mother and boss are too obvious, so let's say the answer is her gynecologist. Maybe he or she is too talkative at the wrong moment or too nosy about her personal life. Whatever the case, once again, it's likely that you've provided yourself a scene in the script. If nothing else, it makes you wonder why she doesn't switch doctors.

I cannot stress enough how useful bios can be in the development of your characters. I recognize that the natural impulse, especially for newer writers who don't know any better, is to just jump right in and get started. You might finish your script that way and you may even get it done weeks or even months faster, but will it be as good? Don't you think a bit of extra effort might lead to a vastly superior result?

Take the time to write bios for your protagonist, antagonist, the 1 supporting character you've chosen to really make great, and perhaps 2 or 3 additional characters that really matter to your story. This process need not take a lot of time and the best part is a bio is never done and can always change. There are no rules. If you initially want your protagonist to be liberal and vegetarian, there's nothing that prevents you from changing that to conservative carnivore if that works better as your story evolves. At least ask the questions and give your characters a chance at real personality, rather than banal descriptions and stereotypical behavior.

KEYS TO REMEMBER

- Making the audience care about your characters is the #1 priority for any and all screenwriters. If readers are indifferent to them, they have no interest in your story and will move on to someone else's script.
- There are a variety of methods by which this can be achieved and they need not all be positive. A great villain is a priceless commodity.
- Most films focus on an external struggle. Make sure to include at least one major internal struggle as an obstacle that must be overcome. Remember, resolving the core conflict should be an epic challenge and compelling internal struggles are frequently a means to achieve this.
- The protagonist of any film is more than likely facing the most substantial and harrowing conflict of their life. As with any real person, such an ordeal MUST have an effect on them. Character change is an absolute necessity to any successful script. If your protagonist is essentially the exact same person at the end of your story as they were in the beginning, you've failed.
- The more the audience can personally identify with or relate to one or more of your characters and the challenges they are facing, the more successful you will be.
- Don't have all your characters, especially friends or allies, always get along. Conflict breeds interest.
- Make sure at least one of your supporting characters is truly special and brings something unique and interesting to your script.
- Do character bios for your major characters. It results in far greater authenticity, less cliché and stereotype, and ultimately more fully realized individuals.

WRITING EXERCISE: Psych 101

There is no better exercise to help you learn about character development than to actually create a bio for one of the central figures in your current or next screenwriting effort. It need not be the protagonist, though that would be a logical place to begin. Whether you prefer to work on a computer or go long hand with a legal pad, the process is the same. Just start asking yourself questions and watch as a unique personality takes shape.

One approach is to go by category. Begin with basic biographical data. Age, sex, where they were born, where they grew up, and where they presently reside. From there, move on to family. Do they have siblings? Parents... alive or dead? Marital status. Big or small extended family. What are the family dynamics?

As you continue, just hit all the major categories. Here are a few to consider:

- Education
- Friends
- Religion
- Politics
- Health
- Sex Life or Habits
- Criminal Record

- Diet/Food Issues
- Sports, Leisure, Hobbies
- Sense of Humor
- Taste in clothes, toys, etc....
- Quirks
- Fears and Phobias

These are just a few areas of concentration. The list provided earlier in this chapter has a number of questions you can ask. Add to it. Think about yourself, those you're close to, and certainly those you dislike or avoid. What makes you trust your best friend? What makes you love your husband? What attracted you to your first love? Who is the most annoying person you've ever met and why?

In addition, while facts are both helpful and necessary to this profile or bio, also give consideration to motives and more abstract examples of personality. What pushes the character's buttons? What turns them on or off? What engages their interest? What or who would they die for … kill for? Are they a dog or cat person? Are they charitable with time and money or oblivious to those in need?

The key to a bio is to just keep asking questions until a fully formed personality comes into focus. The more information you have, the easier it becomes to determine how they will react to any particular situation and what their dialogue should sound like. Don't forget, a bio is never finished so don't feel like you should or should not stop at any given point.

BONUS WRITING EXERCISE:
A PASSIONATE DEFENSE

One of the more challenging tasks a writer has when crafting villains, evil doers, ne'er do wells, misanthropes, and just your average, everyday baddie is to humanize them. The natural instinct is to make evil obvious and very black and white. Motives are pure... which is to say, purely evil. There tends to be very little ambiguity with regards to motive, despite the fact that the very best antagonists are the ones with depth and substance. They have a deeper reasoning to explain their actions and while that explanation may be meaningless to everyone else, it justifies their actions in their own minds at least.

The goal of this exercise is to force you to make your antagonist feel authentic, rather than simply being the simplistic embodiment of evil.

Even the devil has his reasons.

So with that being said, I am making you, at least for a short time, a lawyer. My apologies. Now defend your client...

Write a closing argument in defense of your antagonist. Explain, and more importantly, try to justify their actions.

Attempt to illustrate for the jury what their frame of mind was as they committed their misdeeds. What motivated them and why they may regret their actions? If regret is not an applicable emotion, perhaps you can offer up some mitigating circumstances to help shed light on their behavior in the hope of leniency from the court. See if you can't tip the scales of justice in your client's favor.

Hopefully, when you are finished with this exercise, you'll have something far more valuable than a bio... an engaging backstory and explanation that will make your antagonist infinitely more compelling than the very straightforward black hat often offered up.

CHAPTER 4

The Great Opening…
Dictate the Experience

If you are sitting in a film school class or learning a purely academic approach to screenwriting, you will be told that the primary goal of your opening scene is to engage your audience and invest them in the characters and plot. Sounds simple, right? Here's the twist. For aspiring screenwriters attempting to break in to the industry, you need to understand that agents, managers, producers, executives, and the many assistants and readers who will be responsible for evaluating your work aren't obligated to give you the full 90 to 120 pages to make your case. Actually, it's quite the opposite.

These individuals spend 90% of their day on existing clients and projects. That's where they either already have their money invested or where they will be getting their next paycheck from. That leaves 10% for you and everyone else like you. 10% of their time to find new and exciting voices obscured amidst the pile of mostly lousy work. It's like the one professional singer waiting with a Rose Bowl full of *American Idol* wannabes. While it's crucial that pages 34, 67, and 92 are well done, if you don't capture their attention in the first 5, that won't matter because they won't continue reading long enough to reach those pages.

As many scripts as industry professionals read, I promise you they are fully capable of telling whether one is worth their time as early as page 1 and often by page 5 or 6. So what does that mean? Simply stated, your opening scene is the ONLY one you can be sure will be read by anyone!

Think about that. You have or will spend months, if not years, writing a complete screenplay, and only the first scene is guaranteed to be read. While that may not sound like good news, it really shouldn't be a problem if you resolve yourself to making your opening scene fantastic and force whomever is reading to continue doing so. Even for the most established screenwriters, film is not a medium that does well with slow beginnings. There will always be exceptions, but imagine sitting in a theater and not really feeling engaged by the movie for the first 15 or 20 minutes. Does that sound like a positive cinematic experience? Better to learn the importance of a great opening scene now and not have to worry.

Your opening scene doesn't need to be filled with explosions and gunfire to captivate. It can be nothing but dialogue, as long as it forces the reader to keep going because they can't live without knowing what follows in scene 2.

As an example, look at the film *Inglourious Basterds*. For the most part, the scene is a very straightforward conversation between Colonel Landa and the French farmer who is hiding Shosanna and her family under the floorboards. The subtext is fantastic, as are the performances, though that isn't really important beyond the fact that actors are only as good as their material. It is subtle, nuanced, and brilliant, while leaving the audience desperate for more. Who is this SS Colonel? What becomes of Shosanna? Who are the Basterds?

Another dialogue-heavy scene is the opening of *The Social Network*. Mark Zuckerburg sits in a bar, talking to his date. The scene brilliantly conveys Zuckerberg's personality. His unfiltered rudeness and lack of social grace, not to mention a few beers, ruin the night. The fallout becomes a primary reason for his building Facebook, one of the largest companies in the world, simply so he can "friend" Erica and prove he's not such an asshole.

One of the great opening scenes of all time is in the film *Sunset Boulevard*. Police speed into the driveway of a mansion and race around to the pool in the back where a body is floating. A narrator explains that there has been a murder. The victim is a screenwriter of relative insignificance. So many questions exist in the mind of the reader or audience as the action cuts six months earlier when the story really began. Who is the victim? Why were they murdered? It's a brilliant and captivating beginning, which should be your goal as well.

Regardless of whether you are an aspiring screenwriter, well established, or somewhere in between, the value of immediately engaging your reader, and by extension your audience, cannot be overstated. Capture their attention with a spellbinding opening scene, thereby ensuring their continued interest past the 5th page or the 10th minute.

What do you want the reader to be thinking and feeling at the beginning of your story? **SET THEIR MOOD!** Should they be turned on? Grossed out? Perhaps they have a sense of impending doom. Do you want to create sympathy for your protagonist? Maybe some intense action, tragedy, or outrageous comedy is required. What can you do to convey these or other emotions in your opening? You need them to feel a certain way and you need for that to occur quickly so don't waste time. Dive in and make it happen. Anything less is a waste of paper because if you haven't firmly secured my interest by page 5, your script is already in a world of trouble.

One way to facilitate this agenda is to limit the exposition. Tarantino and Sorkin are two of the greatest writers in the world so that's a high bar. If you can reach it, wonderful; I look forward to seeing you accept your Oscar. If not, consider focusing more on tone, character, and most especially, generating questions. Force the reader to want to know more about the who, what, and when. Depending on the genre, it is also advisable to begin by immediately delivering the core expecta-

tions of your audience. If you are writing an action movie, the opening scene should be action packed. Bond films start that way for a reason!

DON'T BE PASSIVE – DICTATE THE EXPERIENCE!

A few key points to keep in mind:
- Who is your audience?
- Genre — What are the expectations?
- Tone — What mood must be set?
- Pacing — Do you need an explosive beginning or a slow burn?

Generate questions!
- Who is he?
- Will she live?
- Where are they going?
- Who's he chasing?
- What did they do?
- Why was he killed?
- Who's in the trunk?
- Why is there an elephant in the lobby?
- Why are they crying?

Doing so engages your reader and requires they continue reading if they want answers.

KNOW YOUR JOB!

This is a concept I will go into much greater detail on later in this text, but as it specifically pertains to the execution of the opening scene, it needs to be addressed here as well.

All too often, scripts, particularly from aspiring screenwriters (who either think they know better or are copying production drafts or other reprinted material) submit work that wastes time doing other people's jobs. Also, worse than the wasted effort is the potential to offend or annoy those whose job it may be and who might be the one reading your work.

You are the screenwriter, **NOT** the director, lead actor, casting director, or music supervisor. Do your job, not theirs. Don't pick a song because unless the movie is called *Sea of Love*, you're not likely to get your wish and that one has been taken. There is an entire business of music rights, publishing, and licensing that you aren't aware of. Every time a screenwriter declares that "Let It Be" or "Crazy in Love" is playing over the opening credits, you're adding six or even seven figures to the budget. Not your job!

For that matter, neither is identifying where the credits roll. Maybe they appear in the beginning and maybe not, but in either case, it won't be your call. Trust that the credits will be there and your name will be among them.

Don't tell me it's a medium shot or to crane in to a close up. The director will determine how the film is shot. Final Draft software may include transitions like Iris In or Smash Cut, but they exist because the software is used not just for spec drafts, but also shooting scripts and final production drafts that will include input from the director, among many others.

Don't be this writer:

```
FADE IN:

INT. BOOTSIE'S BAZAAR - DAY

BOHEMIAN RHAPSODY plays as we crane in to reveal two
alligators playing tug of war with a jump rope.
Suddenly, a Tom Cruise like male appears. Meet BOOMER
WINSLOW.

                                      MATCH CUT TO:
```

Tell me a story and trust or hope (fingers crossed) that the director will choose how best to shoot it and make it a visual experience worthy of your hard work.

This may not seem like a big deal, but imagine how directors, actors, and others feel when they read scripts at the beginning of the process and the writer is clearly trying to do their job for them. You're not likely to get the reaction you want and it isn't worth the risk of offending someone when none of these things truly enhance or even affect the story in the first place. They are decisions born of vanity and ego and are far better left until later in the process.

If you do your job, the script should speak for and ultimately sell itself.

TYPES OF OPENING SCENES

1. **The Blatant Opening**: Within the first few minutes, you know the hero and/or the villain as well. You may also have a sense of the stakes. Particularly common and effective for action movies. Fast, exciting, and immediately engaging. (Bond films, *The Dark Knight, Star Trek*)

2. **Regular Day**: Life as usual for your protagonist. Everything is very normal, usually until one event occurs to dramatically alter things and often spin everything out of control. (*Cliffhanger, Legally Blonde*)

3. **True Beginning**: The script begins right at the start of the story. The protagonist finds a bag of money or lands in Timbuktu. (*Pretty Woman, Stagecoach*)

4. **Dramatic Irony**: Doesn't generally include the protagonist, but typically involves the reveal of information about or pertaining to the main character that they don't yet know. This opening places the audience in a position of knowledge about the lead and often raises tension as it suggests something is coming. (*The Matrix, Inglourious Basterds*)

5. **Foreshadowing**: Usually involves a looming danger. Typical of doomsday or disaster pictures, as well as horror. (*Independence Day, Armageddon*)

6. **Narrator**: A narrator introduces the story, often providing background on the key characters, politics, or the history of the world we are about to see. This information very often allows us to enter a story in progress. Sometimes the narrator is actually replaced by text on screen such as the famous *Star Wars* crawl. Common to science fiction & fantasy where a mythology is introduced. (*300, Clash of the Titans*)

7. **Montage or Shotgun**: Usually a very fast opening, it is characterized by quick images, sometimes actually of people on screen and sometimes of images such as newspaper headlines that provide necessary backstory. (*Top Gun, The Player*)

8. **Bookends**: Just as it sounds, the film is bookended at the beginning and end with matching scenes. (*The Princess Bride, The Hunt For Red October, Saving Private Ryan*)

Often, a film will incorporate more than one of these such as in *Casablanca*, which begins with a Narrator and then uses a Dramatic Irony open to indicate the travel visas have been stolen and the couriers murdered. *Star Wars* is another example. It begins with the crawl, which is a Narrator opening and is then followed by a combination of a Blatant Opening and Dramatic Irony. There's the immediate action and excitement of Vader's ship attacking Princess Leia's mixed with the reveal that the Death Star plans have been stolen, all of which is information the audience now has, but Luke Skywalker does not.

Bookends, like the Narrator opening, are also used quite often in concert with one of the others. For example, in the film *Saving Private Ryan*, most people remember the epic D-Day landing and subsequent battle as the film's opening scene. However, it actually employed bookends, beginning and ending in the present day with Matt Damon's character, grown old and visiting the Normandy cemetery with his family.

There is no right or wrong style of opening. This list is provided as a guide and for your own understanding. The one caveat I would repeat from earlier is that it is advisable for you to feature the primary expectation of your audience in the opening scene, and doing so might make the decision of what type to employ easier, if not obvious.

So, for example, an action movie should begin with something exciting, just as a comedy should be funny. A drama will likely be more dialogue heavy and focus on introducing one or more of the principal characters while science fiction will establish a setting and a mythology. Beyond that advice, the choice is yours.

KEYS TO REMEMBER

- If you are unknown to the industry, you very likely have only a few scenes and/or pages to engage interest in your work. Your opening scene MUST be exceptional. It must be intriguing and demand the reader keep going lest they miss something special.

- Dialogue tends not to be the strength of less experienced screenwriters and yet most of their opening scenes have an overabundance of it. This generally results in long, often confusing, and frequently boring openings that ruin any chance of your reader going past page 5 or 10. You are most often best served by focusing on plot, humor, excitement, and meeting the core expectations of your audiences in the opening scene until your proficiency allows for more nuanced storytelling.

- Take the reins and set the mood you need your audience to be in. Don't be vague or casual about it. Dictate the experience.

- Generate questions. Create a scene that has readers demanding to know who, what, where, when, or how. That's what keeps them reading!

- As you are writing a spec script, focus on your job alone. Don't worry about credit sequences, song selection, casting, shooting angles, or anything else that is not your responsibility and irrelevant to the quality of your script.

WRITING EXERCISE: LET'S GET IT STARTED

The following exercise will assist in learning how to introduce characters with an air of mystery so as not to give away too much, too soon. In addition, it is designed to help you create a dynamic situation, and most importantly generate questions in the mind of the reader.

You are going to write a scene of 3–5 pages in length.

The main character is your real-life best friend. Go online, pick a city at random, and select a unique location in that city. It can be a landmark like Mt. Rushmore, something a little farther away like the hovercraft terminal in Hong Kong or perhaps lounging on a beach in Tahiti. Sky's the limit.

Now write a scene that features your protagonist. Being that he or she is based on your real friend, you should be able to easily describe and anticipate their actions. Have them quickly come into contact with a mysterious stranger. Regardless of genre, an element of mystery is an easy way to generate questions and foster interest.

Decide ahead of time the genre of film that this scene would be the opening for and use the lessons learned from that chapter to complement your effort. If it's for an action movie, your main character may dodge an attack from the mysterious stranger and chase them as they then try to get away. Your best friend may be dressed as a clown if it's a comedy, though that could just as easily be the start of a horror movie too. Maybe it's a thriller and they witness the stranger committing a crime. Perhaps the stranger is a woman on a bike who the main character hits with his car at the beginning of a romantic comedy.

When you're done, read the scene and make note of all the potential questions that have been suggested by the scene. The who, what, why, and so forth… If there aren't at least a few, consider what changes you could make to fix that.

Key to this exercise is to write this as though it is the opening scene of a new screenplay. Make sure the pages elicit paranoia, intrigue, romance, action, and/or some other emotion that would engage an audience. If you are successful, your best friend will want to know what happens to them. You never know, it might inspire a new idea for your next screenplay. Just make sure you change the names to protect the innocent.

CHAPTER 5

The Second Act...
Ride the Rollercoaster

Act 2 is where most of the action and drama take place in your script. It's where your characters grow and evolve, as well as where they overcome whatever obstacles stand between them and reaching the Climax in Act 3. It is also, by far, the most difficult section to develop, as it is the least clear at the outset of the screenwriting process.

The Second Act is the length of Acts 1 and 3 combined. The main purpose of Act 1 is to introduce characters and setup story while Act 3 is largely about the resolution of conflict. Therefore, you are left with Act 2 as the meat of your script. More than any other part of the screenplay, this is where you must be a storyteller.

When the light bulb goes off and you say to yourself, as we all do, that you have a great idea for a movie, it consists primarily of large chunks of your First Act including one or more principal characters, a setting, and probably both the Inciting Incident and First Act Break that make up the setup and hook of the film. It may or may not include the Climax, but what it **NEVER** includes is a single Second Act scene. That's what makes Act 2 such a challenge and generally, what separates working screenwriters from the rest of the pack.

Sometimes this comes in the form of a structural error where the writer doesn't end Act 1 until somewhere in the 40s or 50s and then follows that with a Second Act that is often half as long as it should be. Sometimes it's just poor story development stemming from a lack of outlining and creativity. People hurry to complete a script without stopping to consider whether writing the words Fade Out is more important than the quality of the work.

Of all the many errors and omissions that aspiring screenwriters make, the most glaring of all and the one most indicative of their amateur status is the failure to deliver a professional Second Act.

ESCALATION

One of the key attributes of a successful Second Act is a series of obstacles and challenges that your protagonist must face and overcome in order to resolve the core conflict. If they were to just skip ahead to the Climax and resolve the conflict easily and with little effort, that wouldn't make for a particularly exciting movie. You just can't have a beginning and an end with no middle. This is remedied by sending your protagonist on a grand cinematic journey. Odysseus was gone 20 years from Ithaca, away from home and family. If he had made it home for dinner, we wouldn't still have to read about him in high school.

Imagine that your Second Act is a series of events, some bringing success and hope, while others are setbacks that diminish a character's spirit. It's a rollercoaster of emotions, up and down and back again. That's what you need to achieve. Another somewhat common mistake made largely by less experienced screenwriters is that the obstacles faced in the Second Act feel very repetitive. Rather than having a series of unique, creative challenges, the protagonist faces what feels like the same obstacle, again and again; while their approach may vary, this situation screams of a lack of development and weak execution.

The barriers and obstacles that present themselves must be more and more dramatic as the story progresses. Much as the characters are expected to change and evolve, for better or worse, the story must as well. Peaks and valleys are necessary for an effective Second Act. Bigger action, higher stakes, increased tension, more to lose, more to gain, heightened emotions are all examples of this. How the story escalates depends substantially on, among other things, the genre and expectations of the audience.

Without this consistent escalation … without ever increasing emotion, a script is stagnant and ultimately boring like a monotone voice calling out, "Bueller? Bueller? Bueller?" Don't put your reader to sleep!

AN EARLY COMPLICATION

In almost all cases, the First Act Break will be an emotional high. It's possible and even likely that it occurs amidst somber or unpleasant circumstances, such as in *Star Wars*, when Luke resolves to travel with Ben and join the rebellion in the wake of his aunt and uncle's murder and the destruction of their farm. Despite this, it is an emotional high because the protagonist is accepting a call to arms … choosing to fight, to press forward in an effort to resolve the core conflict, in this case the destruction of the Death Star.

Given that the start of the Second Act is an emotional high, it stands to reason that shortly thereafter, a valley must appear to draw the emotions downward and thus you have the beginnings of your rollercoaster. This is accomplished by the inclusion of an Early Complication. It will unfold roughly 10–15 pages into Act 2. Typically, coming out of the First Act Break, the protagonist will take their initial steps forward. It's also likely that one or more characters will need to be introduced or addressed in some fashion and it takes a bit of time before you can introduce the first setback. That's what the Early Complication is, a setback for the protagonist in his or her effort to resolve the core conflict.

Previously, I used the example of the brilliant Early Complication present in *Back to the Future*. Another example is in *Silence of the Lambs* when Buffalo Bill takes his next victim hostage. That, in and of itself, would be a significant complication, however, it's exacerbated by the fact that she is also the daughter of a US Senator. The FBI, Jack Crawford, and Agent Starling would be looking to catch him regardless, but the fact that Bill has taken another woman makes finding him quickly all the more vital. A life now hangs in the balance. Add to that the political pressure and media attention that comes as a consequence of whom he's taken and there's substantially more pressure on the investigation.

In *Aliens*, the very obvious Early Complication is the failure of the initial attempt to locate and rescue the missing colonists. The Marines take heavy casualties, their lieutenant freezes and chokes, and the group is ultimately left in far greater danger with a lethal enemy hot on their heels.

Another example is in the classic film *In the Heat of the Night*. It is essentially a whodunit focusing on the murder of a prominent businessman in tiny Sparta, Mississippi. At the outset of Act 2, Detective Virgil Tibbs has been cleared as a suspect and another man has been apprehended. The local cops are sure he's the killer since he was caught with the victim's wallet. However, if he were guilty, there wouldn't be much of movie and thus the Early Complication. Virgil can prove the man's innocence, meaning they still need to identify and catch a killer.

The key to remember is that your protagonist has just engaged the core conflict. Your job as screenwriter is to make that an incredibly daunting challenge. The Early Complication is the first roadblock in their path towards resolution.

THE FIRST CULMINATION

Sometimes, as in the previous examples of *Midnight Run* and *Jerry Maguire*, the Early Complication is in the form of a First Culmination. It's basically just an Early Complication with the addition of the protagonist appearing to successfully resolve the core conflict first, only to have the rug pulled out from beneath them and suddenly being in even worse shape than when they started.

In the film *Taken*, the First Act Break ends with a simple phrase, "Good luck." Liam Neeson races to Paris, but doesn't yet have any leads except for knowing his daughter's kidnappers are Albanian sex traffickers. He needs clues and finds Kim's camera phone, which provides a photograph of Peter, the guy from the airport who set the girls up. Peter is killed after being confronted by Neeson. He's back to square one, with no lead and no obvious next step to find the men who have his daughter, until he reaches out to a former French spy who can help.

Look at the First Culmination as 1 step forward and 2 steps back. Don't forget that while your script should possess an Early Complication, it needn't be in the form of a First Culmination. It's not better, just different, so don't pressure yourself to utilize this option unless it is what best suits your specific story.

THE MIDPOINT

Much as it sounds, the Midpoint occurs roughly at both the midpoint of Act 2, as well as the whole script. I generally reference the need for it to be a game changer because in addition to being the next moment when you can create a significant peak or valley in the plot, it occurs roughly halfway through the story at a time when you should do something to shake things up and reinvest your reader or audience in the journey they are taking with you.

Sometimes it's called *The Reversal*, but I avoid that moniker because the Midpoint doesn't always represent a reversal for the protagonist. Regardless, it is yet another opportunity to introduce chaos, raise tension, alter the course of events, or simply make the resolution of your core conflict more daunting.

Imagine the rollercoaster again. With the First Act Break, emotions are at a peak, then they come screaming downward with the Early Complication around page 35–45. This gives you about 10–15 pages/ minutes to have your characters press forward and slowly head back up to another peak. Now as you approach the Midpoint, around page 45–60, it's time for another rapid descent into an even deeper valley.

Perhaps it is a setback stemming from an emotional handicap of some sort. It could be the addition of a ticking clock or the revelation of new information that makes a situation more dangerous. Maybe it's a shocking death, an ally's betrayal, or some other major development. Bottom line ... your reader and audience are halfway through and you don't want them thinking about the bathroom, Tuesday's meeting, picking up their kid from Benji's house, or anything else. You want their focus fully on your story and the Midpoint affords you an opportunity to hold their attention with the reveal of a game-changing event. It's time to kick it up a notch!

In *The Proposal*, the Midpoint has the couple agreeing to marry in Alaska, over the weekend. This is a dramatic shift that ratchets the drama up to a whole new level for both characters. They had just been faking an engagement, but now they are actually going to have to get married in a matter of days and moreover, in front of Ryan Reynolds' family.

In *The Hangover*, the game-changing Midpoint is the reveal by Mr. Chow that Doug isn't just missing, he's been taken hostage and won't be returned unless the guys come up with 80 thousand dollars. Given that the wedding is 24 hours away, this presents a formidable new challenge.

Just in case you're looking for an example from a more serious, dramatic film, consider *The Godfather*. In that classic, the Midpoint comes when Michael, the son who was never supposed to be part of the family business, murders the duplicitous Sollozzo and his cohort, Captain McCluskey. The ramifications of his actions are tremendous, including his having to flee the country for an extended period while tensions and police pressure die down.

In all of these examples, note that the Midpoint is a dynamic event that provides new energy in the face of even more substantial obstacles and challenges that must be faced and overcome in order to resolve the core conflict.

THE LOW POINT AKA THE SECOND ACT BREAK

The Second Act will culminate in your protagonist's emotional low point. All hope appears to be lost. Any chance of success seems bleak. This plot point is when your protagonist faces the greatest adversity psychologically and/or emotionally because it is the decision to soldier on and push forward, despite the overwhelming odds that leads you into Act 3, and ultimately to your Climax. This is by far the deepest valley in a Second Act that will hopefully be filled with several high peaks and low valleys.

A few examples include Obi-Wan Kenobi's death in *Star Wars*, the Ghostbusters getting thrown in jail, a member of the team having to sacrifice themselves in *Armageddon*, Ryan Hurst's car accident in *Remember the Titans*, and the breakup in *Jerry Maguire*.

An important reminder — in the case of a film that has an emotionally down Climax, one that ends tragically or in defeat, the low point or Second Act Break and the Climax are reversed tonally.

What that means is that in most films, the Second Act Break is the emotional low point and the Climax is the high point, where your protagonist resolves whatever conflict they engaged in the First Act Break. When you have a Climax that ends in defeat, death, or tragedy, that is now the emotional low point. Therefore, the Second Act Break reverses, suggesting the protagonist will be triumphant, only to find in Act 3 that they are not. Go back to the image of peaks and valleys. If the Climax is a peak, you must rise from a valley to generate the greatest degree of excitement and satisfaction. Conversely, if the

Climax is a valley, the opposite would apply and you'd need to approach it from a peak.

The film *Castaway* provides an example of that switch taking place resulting from a failure to resolve the core conflict, which is not surviving the island, but getting back to Helen Hunt. In fact, Hanks' last words to Hunt's character, just before boarding his doomed flight, are "I'll be right back!" Despite enduring years of brutal isolation in the hopes of reuniting with his lost love, circumstances still prevent Hanks from being with her upon his safe return. They've missed their moment. She's remarried with a baby and what might have been, can no longer be, this despite her declaration that Hanks is the love of her life. As a result of this emotional low, the Second Act Break must be a peak: Tom Hanks is rescued at sea and years of struggle and torment are finally over.

There isn't a right or wrong here. It is simply a case of most films having an emotionally positive ending because that is generally more in line with people's hopes, expectations, and desires for their entertainment. People like happy endings and good conquering evil. That's natural. When that is not the case and good doesn't prevail, love doesn't conquer all, and victory is not achieved, the Second Act Break and Climax switch directions to elicit a reversed emotional reaction.

DON'T MAKE IT EASY

Easy is boring. It means there isn't a challenge, and therefore nothing very compelling about the conflict, at the heart of your screenplay. The protagonist's primary and secondary tactics, employed to overcome your core conflict, should **FAIL**, forcing a reassessment of strategy. This is by far the best way to ensure a satisfying Second Act and conflict worthy of the effort.

One of the typical shortcomings of weak scripts from new writers is an impatience to reach the Climax. This is often in evidence by an abbreviated Second Act that's short because success comes too quickly and with minimal exertion by the protagonist. Failure breeds sympathy. It instills an underdog spirit and gets the audience behind the protagonist. Additionally, it fosters the need for ingenuity to solve whatever problems exist. The harder they work for success, the more gratifying it will be to them and to your audience.

As you work to crack your Second Act and devise the many scenes that will comprise it, one place to begin is by thinking of at least 2 or even 3 tactics your protagonist might use to resolve the core conflict and then have them fail. What will they do in response to that? How will they react? Failure cultivates character, in real life as much as in movies so don't let your protagonist succeed too easily, not just in resolving the core conflict, but in overcoming the many smaller challenges he or she will face on the road to the Climax.

A further point to pay special attention to is the fact that audiences loathe coincidence! I cannot emphasize this enough as it is one of the most common screenwriting mistakes, even among professionals. If a character gets EXACTLY what they need, EXACTLY when they need it, the eyes in the theater start rolling and everyone starts groaning. It is also the surest sign that you, as the screenwriter, either didn't take the time to figure out a more creative way of achieving a goal or did and just couldn't come up with anything so you settled for fast over effective.

As a movie fan, you certainly know what I'm referring to so take pains to avoid it in your own material. Don't allow luck to play a consistent role in your writing. Make your characters work for what they need and earn what they receive.

As a general rule, I tell people that audiences will accept one coincidence and perhaps, if they are enjoying the other aspects of the work, forgive a second, but if you exceed that limit, you will more than likely lose their interest.

DON'T BE VAGUE OR PASSIVE

Bottom line, audiences appreciate and require, even if they don't realize it, specificity. The devil is in the details. Your primary conflict must be clearly identified.

No one wants to spend the Second Act watching your protagonist stumble along hoping to be a success in who knows what or wishing for love to magically come their way. They don't want to watch a team that merely wants to win, but rather, is risking blood, sweat, and tears to beat the Russians or to win the national title. There's a reason the movie *Miracle* is about the semi-final game versus the Soviet Union and not the actual gold medal winner against Finland. Beating the Russians was the miracle and thus the movie; winning gold was just a formality.

Great films have very detailed, well defined plots. They don't meander, they don't vacillate, and they don't appear indecisive. To be clear, the need for detail has nothing to do with the reveal of information or the effort that might be made to create mystery or suspense with twists and unexpected turns.

Amidst the uncertainty that might exist for a character who doesn't yet have all the answers, there will still always be a VERY specific agenda, a mission, and probably several goals. Your script can't hope to engage a reader with vague impressions about wanting victory or finding a soul mate. It isn't enough to say Bob wants to find love. You need to have Bob wanting to find love with Rachel because she's so ... You fill in the rest!

The protagonist must defeat a **specific** foe or achieve success in a **specific** battle. He or she must attract **that** guy or **that** girl, not just a guy or a girl. Additionally, don't have five different things that have to happen in the Climax. A core conflict is a singular issue, which isn't to say you can't have subplots and lesser setups that require resolution, but the core conflict is one very specific issue to be resolved. Identify it and make sure your audience is clear and engaged.

FILLING IN THE BLANKS – CONFLICT

As you begin to develop your Second Act and work out its content, keep this in mind … conflict is drama and drama, regardless of genre, is necessary for your success. Whatever the hook of your film and the primary conflict setup in the First Act Break, there should be a series of smaller goals and/or obstacles that need to be faced, conquered, overcome, and otherwise thwarted along the way.

Resolving the core conflict of your film MUST be a multistep process!

It should not be accomplished easily or in one action. A long, winding, up and down road to success will make your film significantly more enjoyable and entertaining.

Here are 3 questions to aid you in creating conflict:

1. List 5 things that could potentially make your protagonist's resolution of the core conflict more challenging. Some sort of handicap, an ally betrays them, they lose something crucial like a map or a key, they need to locate someone vital like a glass blower or an expert forger, etc.

2. Who, other than the antagonist, could make your protagonist's journey more difficult? Perhaps it's only in one scene, but that's not a negative. You already have an antagonist and don't need another one. For example, in *Pretty Woman*, the bitchy salesperson who won't help Julia Roberts or the landlord she has to avoid because she doesn't have the rent. In both cases, these relatively insignificant characters help to advance the plot.

3. Beyond what you may have already considered, devise 5 ways in which the protagonist might suffer if they fail to resolve the core conflict.

The following are definitions for the types of conflict that can exist in your story:

INNER CONFLICT: The most difficult to dramatize because it largely consists of a character's internal demons and emotions and therefore you must find ways to demonstrate visually how this internal strife affects the character, as well as others around him or her. Examples include chemical dependency, lack of confidence, fears, urges, abandonment issues, guilt, etc.

RELATIONAL CONFLICT: The most common form of conflict; it is the drama that exists between two or more characters. Examples include cop versus crook, infidelity, fight over politics, a coach dealing with a player, a mother punishing her daughter for missing curfew, a lawyer questioning a hostile witness, etc.

SITUATIONAL CONFLICT: This is the conflict that exists between an individual and a situation such as a battle against cancer, a struggle to survive a sinking ship, escaping an erupting volcano, etc.

SOCIETAL CONFLICT: The conflict that exists between an individual and a large group such as racism, gender rights, social injustice, religious freedom, etc.

A screenplay can and very well may incorporate many or all of the above conflicts and perhaps more than one of a certain kind. Any effective script will certainly have at least one internal and external struggle. More often than not, unless the internal problem of your protagonist is the plot or focus of your film, it will be something that affects his or her ability to resolve the external one.

Going back to the example *Pretty Woman*, the core conflict may be Richard Gere and Julia Roberts living happily ever after, but along the way, Edward must come to terms with his commitment issues (internal), he must makeover Vivian (societal), get jealous of the attention another man pays her (internal/relational), deal with his sleazy attorney (relational), and contend with the business deal that has brought him to LA (situational), to name but a few.

Note that each of these also furthers the plot, as all elements in a script should. The makeover, in addition to being a source of comedy, advances both characters. The jealousy shows that the relationship has grown beyond a business transaction and actual feelings are now involved. The business deal and Edward's altered intentions for Ralph Bellamy's company highlight the change Vivian has inspired in him.

Let's look at *Top Gun*. Beyond the core conflict, Maverick must contend with the complication that Charlie is one of his instructors and although it's not his fault, he also feels responsible and guilty for his best friend's death. This guilt exacerbates his already tenuous lack of confidence derived from the murky facts surrounding his father's death. Add to all of that a rivalry with Ice and you've got a lot of conflict to drive the plot before reaching resolution in Act 3.

To reiterate, conflict is drama and drama, regardless of genre, is absolutely necessary for your success.

Creating Subplots

No movie can survive without at least one or more secondary story-lines. If for no other reason than they provide you a place to go when you need a transition, but more importantly, they elevate the drama and create added opportunities for action, comedy, romance, or any number of complimentary elements to whatever story you are telling. Further, as has previously been stated, with multiple internal and external struggles and goals which must be met in order to resolve the core conflict, the natural byproduct is subplots and their inclusion makes the addition of conflict, a vital component of your script, far easier to accomplish.

The most common subplot is a love interest, except in the case of a romantic comedy or love story where that is the primary conflict. It may be a dying parent or friend or perhaps a business deal or a crisis at work. It could be the breakup of the protagonist's marriage or their need to beat an addiction. Quite possibly, you might use several.

Without subplots, your script is likely to be too linear and you will have trouble sustaining interest. Also, you will find the advancement of subplots to be very useful as transitions when you need to cut away from your protagonist. Don't forget also that the development of your subplots will give you much needed content for your Second Act.

Keep in mind, however, that as with supporting characters, a subplot that doesn't add to or enhance the overall story should **NOT** be included. While it may be a funny situation or a cool idea, don't use or keep something that doesn't advance your plot. It can be the best idea you've ever come up with, but if it fails to further your story, save it for something else where it might survive the editing process that would surely cut it away from this effort.

As an exercise, let's take a look at a popular film. In this case, *Good Will Hunting.* The core conflict is a reflection of the title. Making Will Hunting the good guy that he is, but is afraid to be because of his past. It's basically about Will coming to terms with his childhood and the horrible effect it has had on his life in order to realize the enormous potential that resides within him and embrace the future that's possible as a result.

Okay, that's the core conflict ... So what are the subplots? Well, love interests are the most common and that holds true here. Will's relationship with Skylar is a subplot. So is his relationship with Ben Affleck's Chuckie, his best friend and closest confidante. He doesn't really have any one-on-one scenes with Casey Affleck or Cole Hauser, but his overall relationship with his friends as a group is another one.

His work at MIT with Stellan Skarsgard's Professor Lambeau is yet another one. His arrest for assault and subsequent court hearing is as well.

There are others, but let's take a look at how each one contributes to and advances the overall story. Obviously, Will's feelings towards Skylar are a major factor as they reflect the progress or lack thereof, from his therapy sessions with Robin Williams. Similarly, his work with the professor allows him to really step into the world he knows he belongs in, but has thus far only snuck around to visit. The friendship with Chuckie provides Will perspective and serves as a major wakeup call during the scene when they are on a break from the construction site and Chuckie tells Will he's sitting on a winning lottery ticket and it would be an insult to him if Will's still breaking bricks in the future. This is such a pivotal moment that it becomes integral to the Climax as Will leaves for California with no goodbyes, giving Chuckie the exact exit he asked for.

We could spend pages and pages dissecting all of the subplots in that single movie and how each one advanced the overall story, but I believe the point is well made. Subplots are a necessary element of any feature screenplay. Imagine how linear and frankly, boring, your script would be without them.

Many less experienced screenwriters fall into this trap, which is a clear indication not just of poor execution, but a thorough lack of understanding when it comes to narrative storytelling and screen-writing as a profession. This is one of those mistakes that is tantamount to holding up a sign saying you don't belong. Your script will be short and dramatically lacking in creativity, and will quickly find itself in the blue recycle bin, so take the time to flesh out your story and provide it with interesting subplots and alternate perspectives to enhance your final product.

DON'T FORGET THE ANTAGONIST

Another common misstep is the almost total disregard for the antagonist in the Second Act. **Please don't make this mistake**! It's a BIG
one. The Second Act is half your movie, and the villain or antagonist is
quite often the most interesting character. Therefore, you are sacrificing
opportunity, intrigue, suspense, and any number of other things by
excluding them. Cutting to the antagonist also provides you a natural
transition when you need to
step away from your protagonist or other characters.

"It puts the lotion in the basket."

Imagine if we never saw
Darth Vader during the
Second Act of *Star Wars*
or Loki and his messianic
musings in *The Avengers*. If
your antagonist is a worthy
opponent, they rightfully
deserve substantial attention throughout the film, most especially during
Act 2. Can you picture *Silence of the Lambs* without Buffalo Bill in this
infamous scene?

A really helpful way of seeing this is by looking at films where the
antagonist isn't a person, such as *Armageddon* or *Apollo 13*. Think how
those movies would play if throughout Act 2, there was no mention of
the asteroid or the damaged spacecraft. Would either make sense?

Often, what occurs is that writers either rely on henchmen as "bad
guys" during the Second Act, or they simply forget and/or overlook the
antagonist, focusing instead on the main character.

They realize the need to bring the antagonist back in Act 3 for the
resolution of the core conflict, but by that point, it's far too late. Sadly,
many if not most of these writers choose not to go back and fix the
problem, but instead press forward, which is again more evidence of
prioritizing speed over quality.

The audience should relish in their characterization and take pleasure in the scope of their evil or duplicity. Keep in mind that the more audacious your antagonist, the more delicious their machinations, the more of a challenge they represent, and perhaps most importantly, the more omnipresent they are, the more satisfying it will be when your protagonist proves victorious or successful in the conclusion.

THE #1 TIP I CAN GIVE YOU – SO PAY ATTENTION!

It is extremely common for inexperienced screenwriters to sit in front of a blank screen or sheet of paper trying to imagine what their hero should do to progress through the story and in particular, The Second Act, but they struggle mightily for answers, unsure of the particular obstacles they will be facing. How will they catch the killer or beat cancer? How will they win the girl's heart or save the planet from imminent destruction? They suffer from a form of writer's block, the most common type to afflict screenwriters in my opinion.

It's not surprising … they are trying to solve problems they haven't yet devised, looking for answers when they don't know the questions. How do you catch the killer when you don't know what the killer is

doing, where they are, or how they are attempting to avoid capture?

HERE'S YOUR VERY SIMPLE SOLUTION:
GO TO THE DARK SIDE!

Create the problems first and it becomes much easier to conjure up solutions. As you attack the development of Act 2, rather than asking what you or the protagonist would or should do, first put yourself in the position of thinking as the antagonist. Embrace your inner badass and first decide what the antagonist would or should do to stop the successful resolution of the core conflict.

How can they make it harder or more challenging? What steps would they take to impede the resolution? When you begin by imagining what obstacles the antagonist might place in your hero's path, it immediately suggests a series of tactics that must occur to overcome those challenges. Figure out the questions first and coming up with the answers becomes exponentially easier.

Become the villain. Be the devil on your shoulder, not the angel. You often hear actors speak of how much fun it is to play the villain or be a bitch ... Give it a try. You might enjoy the experience.

KEYS TO REMEMBER

- The most difficult section, by far, to develop because it is NEVER part of the original idea. An enormous number of screenwriters falter because they are either too lazy or in a rush and as a result, they fail to sufficiently deliver a competent or creative Second Act. This is one of the most common missteps among screenwriters of all levels of experience.
- The Second Act should be an epic struggle. The protagonist's journey must be arduous and full of challenges with both success and failure along the way, resulting in an emotional rollercoaster that maintains an audience's interest.
- The three major Second Act plot points will naturally lead you to the desired peaks and valleys of emotion, so don't forget to include any of them.
- The most likely point at which an audience will lose interest in your story is halfway through. That's when a bathroom break or a nap will be considered. A game-changing Midpoint to re-engage their interest is your best defense.

- Easy is boring. Don't allow your protagonist to march through the Second Act with relative ease. It makes for a lousy read and a boring film. Failure not only makes things more interesting, it breeds character and strength, as well as the imagination required to overcome.
- Don't be in a hurry to reach the Climax. This often results in an underwhelming and frequently too short Second Act. What's it matter if you finish writing more quickly if the script is mediocre or worse as a result?
- Audiences loathe coincidence. It is a sign of lazy writing and a lack of creativity.
- Just as you must include one or more engaging supporting characters, so too must you craft compelling subplots to deliver a fully formed narrative. However, any subplot you include MUST add to the depth of one or more major characters and/or the core conflict. Unrelated distractions are just that.
- Don't forget to include the antagonist in the Second Act. It is a common mistake and a substantial missed opportunity when they only appear at the beginning and end of a story.
- Don't forget to "Go to the Dark Side" when writer's block or uncertainty becomes a problem. It's much easier to provide answers when you know the questions!

WRITING EXERCISE:
CONFLICT IS A PART OF LIFE

The emergence and resolution of several conflicts will represent a significant portion of your Second Act.

Make a list of 20 conflicts that could emerge as a result of your protagonist engaging the core conflict. 10 of them should be major, as in the death of a friend or suffering a devastating injury. Conversely, the other 10 should be relatively minor and might be resolved in the course of a single scene, such as how to get from point A to point B or needing to find the old phone number of an important witness. Try to include at least 1 of each type of conflict, though Societal may not be applicable to your particular story ... although, perhaps it could be?

Next, devise 3 possible responses and/or solutions to each conflict you've listed. Keep in mind that not all of them, and in fact none of them, need to be successful. Remember, having your protagonist fail in their efforts can be a positive thing for their development and your script.

As an example, in *Raiders of the Lost Ark*, the core conflict is finding the ark. A major conflict would be needing to confront Marion again after so many years or the fact that the Nazis are also looking for the ark as well, while a minor conflict could include how to get from the ship to the submarine or what to do in order not to be killed by the power of the ark in the Climax.

Your Second Act will need an Early Complication, a game-changing Midpoint, an emotional low, not to mention a consistent escalation of the stakes as your plot unfolds. This list will give you several ideas for those beats, as well as the manner in which your protagonist will be in a position to face others. More importantly, facing and overcoming obstacles and resolving multiple conflicts is what makes any film, regardless of genre, a satisfying experience.

Finally, if you've completed the character exercise, your bio should inform you greatly as to how your specific character might respond and react to any given conflict that arises.

CHAPTER 6

The Road Map…
A to B, Not A to Z

There are a number of different methods "the experts" teach with regards to outlining a feature screenplay. The Road Map is the one I created, teach to students, and use myself. I believe that more than anything, it simplifies the process and more importantly, removes the frustration and tension that writers feel while looking at a blank page or screen and feeling overwhelmed by the need to fill a hundred pages.

Movie ideas will always incorporate elements of the First Act including the Inciting Incident and the First Act Break. In some cases, elements of the Climax might be known as well, but they NEVER include the Second Act. No one has a bout of sudden inspiration and conceives the middle of a movie. Screenwriters take an initial idea from concept to execution, but a common problem, particularly for those who lack experience or don't outline, is to bridge the gap between the First Act Break on page 25–30 and the Climax at the very end of the script with minimal thought and few pages. They wrack their brains, trying to connect the two in one flash of genius. **NOT POSSIBLE!**

You cannot conceive 40 or 50 scenes and an hour of content in one miraculous thought and the more you try, the more likely you are to suffer an aneurism.

There are three common outcomes that plague amateur screenwriters who forego outlining. Depending on whether or not you've ever written a script or tried to, one or more of these may sound very familiar.

The first scenario is that you race through the initial 25 or 30 pages. It's easy and fun. You're impressed with yourself for getting so much accomplished in such a short span of time. Well, it's not surprising that you were able to do this because as stated previously, these are the pages where all of your initial thoughts for the Inciting Incident, First Act Break, protagonist, supporting players, and the setting or location would appear. Now it's time to begin Act 2 and suddenly, ummmmm... You have no idea what happens next and get frustrated quickly that you can't figure it out. This leads to your quitting, leaving many lonely First Acts out there with nothing but unresolved conflict.

The second scenario is a strange one because it involves more work. Quite often, writers will soldier through that wall and start working on Act 2. They come up with one or two ideas and then, when they can't think of more, things start to get redundant. I wrote earlier of a situation where writers sometimes repeat themselves in the Second Act. They have the protagonist face what is essentially the same conflict or challenge, only with slight variations. People in this category tend to write, then write some more, and then keep writing for a lot longer.

Suddenly, they have an outlandishly long Second Act. Realizing that they aren't writing *Gone with the Wind*, an abbreviated Third Act is slapped on leading to an overly abrupt Climax and ending. The script may look okay at 130 or more pages, but upon closer inspection, one finds the structure is way off. The Second Act is far too long AND repetitive and the Third Act is surprisingly short. Often, because the final page count may be a little high, but still plausible, writers who fall into this group convince themselves that they've done a good job and move on to sharing the script with an untold number of unlucky readers.

The third scenario is sort of the opposite of the second. Instead of getting repetitive, the writer executes a very short Second Act that typically also involves the protagonist marching through the story with relative ease and minimal challenge. Writers in this category tend to be very conscious of and nervous about script length. They know they should have at least 90 pages. With a Second Act that is suddenly done around page 60, they write the longest Third Act they can muster, stretching it out to about 20 pages or a bit more for a final tally of roughly 80 pages. Sometimes it's as few as 70. In such cases, they convince themselves that movies less than 90 minutes have been released in the past so it must be possible. Alternatively, they make the argument that *close* to 90 pages is close enough. Readers are much more jovial about these scripts as they're quick and easy to breeze through, but that doesn't make them any better.

Like I said, one or more of these scenarios may strike a chord with you, but regardless, these are the extremely common mistakes that plague screenwriters who don't outline. I don't actually know any professional writers that don't outline at least a little, but they have the experience to do some of this work on the fly. If you are new or relatively new to screenwriting, I heartily recommend you take outlining very seriously as the failure to do so will be the most obvious and likely cause of your utter failure to write even a passable screenplay, let alone one worthy of being considered professional by the industry.

The Road Map is designed to force you to think one step at a time, rather than on the whole script. If you are driving cross-country, you don't take just one road or make just one turn. You are traveling from A to B, not A to Z, and a script is no different. You may be going from Los Angeles to New York, but you have to get to Barstow first, not to mention passing through Arizona, Texas, Oklahoma, and several more states along the way. Alternatively, maybe you go a different route and pass through Utah, Wyoming, and Nebraska, or perhaps a Southern route stopping off in New Orleans? Are you visiting Mt. Rushmore or picking up Cousin Betty in Omaha? In screenwriting, you have multiple options and a long road to travel so plot out the best route and take it one stretch at a time.

In *Raiders of the Lost Ark*, Indiana Jones decides to go after the ark and has one clue — his former mentor, Abner Ravenwood, has the necessary headpiece to the staff of Ra, and his daughter Marion is his only way to find him. Jones must go and see her in Nepal. What does that mean? It indicates the next sequence of events. He must travel to Asia and that's shown as a short montage. Next, Marion is introduced, competing in a drinking game, and finally, Jones enters the bar and confronts her. This, in turn, allows for the reveal of details regarding their romantic history and subsequent break-up. Some conflict is established.

If you were the screenwriter, what would come next? George Lucas and Lawrence Kasdan determined it was time for the Nazis to appear, thus delivering on the audience expectation of some action when the two sides trade gunfire and Marion's bar is burned down. Marion is revealed to have the headpiece and with her bar now destroyed, she declares that she's now Jones' partner. More conflict is injected for the protagonist and the writer knows what must come next. They must travel to Egypt and in so doing, it becomes necessary to introduce the supporting character of Jones' friend, Sallah, played by John Rhys-Davies. One scene begets another and so on.

Let's take a look at a graphic representation of the Road Map to better illustrate how this works.

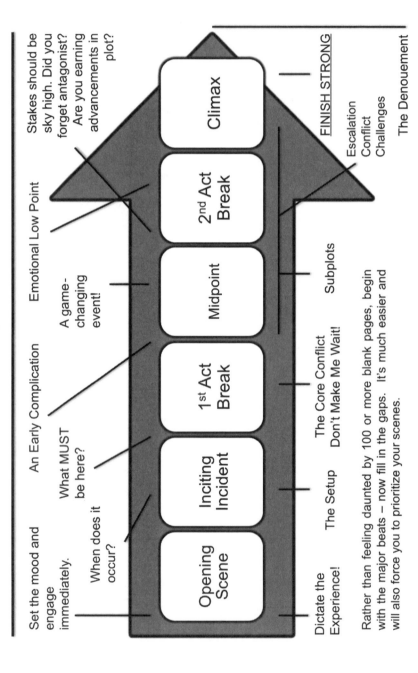

THE ROAD MAP

Set the mood and engage immediately.

An Early Complication

Emotional Low Point

Stakes should be sky high. Did you forget antagonist? Are you earning advancements in plot?

What MUST be here?

A game-changing event!

When does it occur?

FINISH STRONG

Escalation
Conflict
Challenges

The Denouement

Opening Scene

Inciting Incident

1st Act Break

Midpoint

2nd Act Break

Climax

Dictate the Experience!

The Setup

The Core Conflict
Don't Make Me Wait!

Subplots

Rather than feeling daunted by 100 or more blank pages, begin with the major beats – now fill in the gaps. It's much easier and will also force you to prioritize your scenes.

The first thing I want you to take note of are the major beats. They include all seven of the major plot points, two of which are not in boxes, along with the opening scene. That's where you begin. You have an idea for a movie. It very likely includes the Inciting Incident and First Act Break. Now let's assume that while you haven't yet figured out precisely how the protagonist resolves the core conflict, you have a notion of whether they are successful or not, perhaps the location of the Climax, and at least a strong sense of how the film concludes.

Now your mission is to focus not on 100 or more blank pages, but the considerably smaller gaps in between your major plot points; and as you fill in those gaps, the remaining major beats should come into much clearer focus.

Take a look at your First Act Break. Don't worry about anything else for the moment. What is set up? Your protagonist engages the core conflict. That should indicate or at least suggest a likely first step that MUST be taken. What is it? The answer very likely gives you the first scene of your Second Act!

Now that you have that scene, what does it then set up or require comes next? And so on and so forth. The point is that in going one step at a time, looking at what each scene consists of or reveals and more importantly necessitates next, it allows you to fill in the blanks, especially in Act 2.

Moreover, if you look again at the graphic and consider the relative length of a feature script, you'll also realize that instead of an imposing 100 pages of white and no notion of how to fill them, suddenly you have 10- or 15-page sections that are much easier to pack. In fact, whereas it felt like you had more space than you could ever fill before, suddenly you won't have enough for all your ideas. Thus the Road Map has the added benefit of forcing you to prioritize the scenes that truly matter and advance the plot, versus others that sound great in theory but really don't add value to the overall piece.

Here is a version of the Road Map applied to a popular film:

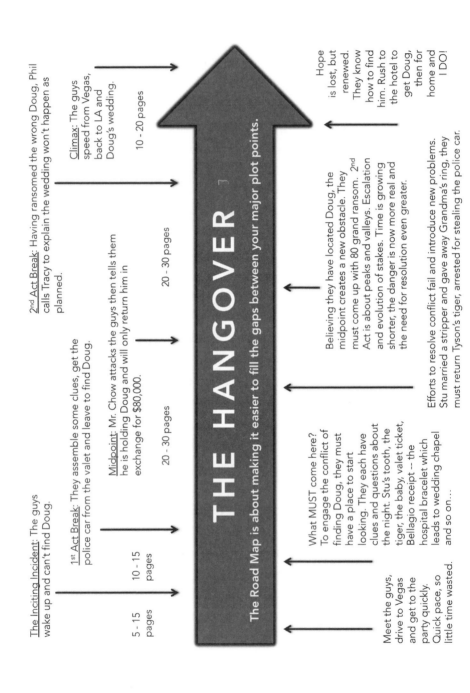

THE HANGOVER

The Road Map is about making it easier to fill the gaps between your major plot points.

The Inciting Incident: The guys wake up and can't find Doug.

1st Act Break: They assemble some clues, get the police car from the valet and leave to find Doug.

Midpoint: Mr. Chow attacks the guys then tells them he is holding Doug and will only return him in exchange for $80,000.

2nd Act Break: Having ransomed the wrong Doug, Phil calls Tracy to explain the wedding won't happen as planned.

Climax: The guys speed from Vegas, back to LA and Doug's wedding.

10 - 20 pages

20 - 30 pages

20 - 30 pages

10 - 15 pages

5 - 15 pages

Meet the guys, drive to Vegas and get to the party quickly. Quick pace, so little time wasted.

What MUST come here? To engage the conflict of finding Doug, they must have a place to start looking. They each have clues and questions about the night. Stu's tooth, the tiger, the baby, valet ticket, Bellagio receipt -- the hospital bracelet which leads to wedding chapel and so on...

Believing they have located Doug, the midpoint creates a new obstacle. They must come up with 80 grand ransom. 2nd Act is about peaks and valleys. Escalation and evolution of stakes. Time is growing shorter, the danger is now more real and the need for resolution even greater.

Efforts to resolve conflict fail and introduce new problems. Stu married a stripper and gave away Grandma's ring, they must return Tyson's tiger, arrested for stealing the police car.

Hope is lost, but renewed. They know how to find him. Rush to the hotel to get Doug, then for home and I DO!

Let's assume your Inciting Incident ENDS on page 15 and your First Act Break BEGINS on page 26. You have 11 pages in between to work with so ask yourself, what MUST occur in those pages? Perhaps a character should be introduced. Maybe the protagonist needs to travel somewhere or acquire something. You might need a scene with the antagonist, an ally, the introduction of an impediment, or the release of new information. Suddenly, you're forced to make decisions about what you can and cannot include, how to reduce something from a 5 page scene down to a third of a page and so on.

Between your First Act Break and the Early Complication, there are at most maybe 15 pages. The gap between your opening scene and Inciting Incident is likely half that. The largest section you'll have to contend with is from the Midpoint to your Second Act Break and even that is at most 25 or 30 pages. Travel from A to B, not A to Z!

Another MAJOR benefit of the Road Map is the prevention of not just a common problem, but one of the most irritating for a reader. An overwhelming number of screenwriters, especially those with less experience, meander in their First Acts, providing far too much exposi-tion and not nearly enough plot. They drone on endlessly about things that either belong in Act 2 or shouldn't be in the script at all. The result of this is a First Act that doesn't end until at  least page 40, if not long after. To give you a sense of just how big a problem this is, imagine sitting in a movie theater for 40 minutes or even a full hour and not yet knowing what the movie is about. Think about it. It's ridiculous!

That's the reality though of not establishing the core conflict prior to page 40 or beyond. Until the protagonist engages that conflict, the audience and/or reader won't know what the movie is about. Would you sit in a theater that long without knowing why?

The Road Map will also help you to notice long stretches that don't meet audience expectations, highlight a supporting player, and avoid forgetting the antagonist and other elements that have been highlighted in this text. Additionally, it simplifies the process in such a way as to diminish the anxiety often experienced when writing a screenplay, especially a first one. It is so much less daunting to crack 10 or 15 pages than try to figure out 100 plus all at once.

KEYS TO REMEMBER

- It is impossible to conceive 50 scenes or 100 pages in a single thought. Writers often fail or give up because they hit a wall while trying to do so. Instead, focus on the spaces between your major beats.
- Use the limited space in a given section to force yourself to prioritize not only what scenes are necessary, but also how long your scenes should be. Sometimes a scene requires multiple pages and sometimes the same information can be presented in a quarter page.
- Use the Road Map to make sure that you don't write a longer than necessary First Act. It is an extremely common error that screenwriters make and results in a reader or audience having to wait far too long to find out what the core conflict is and thus what the movie is about.
- Use the Road Map to illustrate the frequency with which you are delivering on the audience's core expectations, particularly when working in a genre defined by tone and remedy the situation when it indicates you have failed to do so.
- Use the Road Map to make sure you include all of the necessary plot points, highs and lows, and act breaks to arrive at a finished product with the potential to be labeled as professional work.

WRITING EXERCISE: ROAD TRIP!

Presumably, if you are reading this text, you already have an idea for a screenplay you would like to work on. With that in mind, this is less a writing exercise and more a first step towards making that idea into a screenwriting reality.

Now begins your outlining process utilizing the Road Map. Use index cards (my preference), a legal pad, your computer, or the world's biggest whiteboard. How and/or where you outline is your call. Do what makes you feel comfortable. The vital thing to keep in mind as you begin this exercise is that it will not be quick or easy, nor will it ever be complete until your script is, so don't worry about story gaps, indecision, or the potential for better ideas down the road. The gaps will get filled, the indecision will pass, and better ideas will most certainly come.

Begin by identifying as many of the major plot points as you can.

Now start filling in the gaps. What must occur in the pages between your opening scene and the Inciting Incident? What character or characters MUST be introduced? What locations MUST be visited? What information MUST be revealed to the audience? Make a list of the things that need to happen in those pages. Now put those elements into engaging and entertaining scenes.

Continue with the gap between the Inciting Incident and the First Act Break. Then the real heavy lifting will begin with Act 2. Remember that your Second Act should be a rollercoaster ride with peaks and valleys. Mix setbacks with a consistent escalation in drama. Don't forget to have the primary and secondary efforts at resolution fall short or even fail miserably. Develop your protagonist, remember to include your antagonist, and make a supporting character great.

Determine that first Early Complication. Perhaps it comes in the form of a First Culmination or perhaps not, but in either case, you should endeavor to conceive a dynamic obstacle or stumbling block that immediately makes the resolution of the core conflict that much more challenging.

Work on each gap. Feel free to skip around, though it will likely be easier if you work sequentially. It allows you to employ the approach of one scene begets another. Each scene suggests and often necessitates what must come next.

That being said, I guarantee you will have, and perhaps already have had, one or more ideas for scenes you want to include later in the story. Go ahead and place them in your Road Map. The more complete it is, the better; and it is also sometimes more helpful to work in reverse as well. If you know where you want or need to go, figuring out how to get there can be a lot easier.

For the purposes of this exercise, you should try to get as much of the Road Map done as possible, but bear in mind that if you do it right, it will take some time. Since the development of your story isn't complete until your script is, it need not be finished before you actually start writing.

All your best ideas won't come right away. Be open to new options, better alternatives, and more interesting scenarios, but also be mindful of the fact that the Road Map makes outlining substantially less complicated. A thorough outline will make your script better, the process of writing it easier, and your prospects far more appealing. Also remember that you are only halfway through this text and still have more lessons to learn so there should be no hurry to get your Road Map done.

CHAPTER 7

The Great Climax…
The Final Is 50% of Your Grade

Back in high school, did your work in week one or five factor into your grade as much as the final exam? Imagine that you have created a script and the first 90 pages are nothing short of brilliant. A fantastic idea accentuated by richly imagined characters, witty and intelligent dialogue, and a truly creative story. Everything is perfect and then the reader gets to the final 10 or 20 pages and well, they suck. How do you think that reader would perceive the entirety of your script? Obviously, this scenario is exaggerated. However, if the Climax fails to satisfy and doesn't measure up to the quality of the rest of the script and/or movie, then you've really let yourself and the audience down and fallen into a common pitfall of screenwriting plaguing writers at all levels of experience.

What do you think people will be talking about when they put down the script or leave the theater? Do you imagine they will give you credit for the hour and a half where you sufficiently, if not substantially entertained them, or do you suppose they will gripe about the lousy ending? This isn't a glass half full question. It won't matter what the personality of the audience or reader is. If you let them down in the home stretch, all you'll hear is the sound of their utter disappointment. Haven't you exited a film having hated the ending, and that's all you can talk about? It's not uncommon, but it's a killer; for those writers who haven't already broken through, it's more than enough to keep them on the outside, looking in.

No pressure or anything, but just as it's important to immediately engage the reader or audience with a dynamic opening, it is equally vital that you send them off with a smile, thanks to a fully satisfying Climax.

The Climax is all about conflict resolution, but in an exciting and compelling manner. It is and must be the dramatic apex of your script. As such, all forces in opposition will come to a head in this scene or sequence. It is incumbent upon you as the screenwriter to make sure that high point is achieved because anything less than that and you will hear things like *anticlimactic, dull, predictable, boring,* etc....

Don't forget that regardless of genre, your protagonist will be reaching the end of what is likely the greatest struggle of their life, with often very personal stakes. Earn the victory or make the audience really invest in their defeat. Generate an emotional reaction. Make your reader and the audience feel... ANYTHING. Just like indifference is the enemy of character, it is similarly your foe here.

People can be exultant, happy, sad, horrified, angry, and so forth, but what you don't want is for them to be indifferent as that means you've failed to satisfy their hopes and expectations for your Climax and ending. Unfortunately, no matter how effective your work was prior to this point, the conclusion is all that will be on their minds. This is especially worrisome if we're talking about an industry decision maker who holds your screenwriting future in their hands.

This concept is most obvious in an action piece because good and evil face off in what is expected to be the most exciting moment of the movie, but the drama should be present even if Batman isn't battling the Joker. You have asked the reader/audience to care about that struggle and so the payoff must be worthy of that. Whether it is Comedy, Drama, Family, or anything else, the very definition of a movie Climax is the final confrontation of protagonist and antagonist in the ultimate showdown over the core conflict. Blah is not a word that you want associated with the Climax of your script or movie.

Going back to the rollercoaster analogy, imagine a series of ups and downs mirroring the emotional journey of your protagonist; then, just as you are taking them towards the biggest thrill of the ride, the coaster levels out and rolls to a slow and uneventful stop. How does that sound?

Every scene is important and for all sorts of different reasons, but if you're fortunate enough to have someone reading your script all the way through and actually getting to the Climax, consider the ramifications of their final impression of your work being a letdown.

VERY IMPORTANT! TAKE NOTE OF THIS AS IT IS THE ONE **UNBREAKABLE** RULE:

YOUR CLIMAX MUST MATCH YOUR FIRST ACT BREAK!!!

This isn't an option. It's not an artistic choice, nor is it conformist behavior to follow this very simple rule. You're not a rebel if you break it, nor are you a trendsetter or a maverick. It's just bad writing!

In the First Act Break, your protagonist engages a core conflict. They spend the Second Act endeavoring to resolve it and do so, successfully or not, in your Climax. If, however, you have them resolve a completely different conflict, you have negated all the work in your screenplay from the First Act Break. Plus, your story wouldn't make any sense!

Imagine your core conflict is Penelope saving the world from vicious, fire-breathing koala bears. She engages this frightful situation and works to resolve it in Act 2. Now, you reach the Third Act and Climax and the conflict she resolves is catching her no-good, cheatin' louse of a husband, Willie Ray, with

a girl named Bambi. Would that make any sense? Setting aside the resulting confusion, how frustrating would it be not to know if she managed to defeat the evil koalas?

This isn't about happy endings. Emotionally, tonally, creatively… End your script however you'd like, but the conflict you address in your Climax MUST be the conflict you setup in the First Act Break. Even if you don't employ a Three Act Structure, there is still a core conflict engaged early by the protagonist and this rule applies. Failure in this manner is an absolute script killer because when it turns up, the pass is automatic. For this reason, there aren't examples to provide because scripts like this never make it to the big screen. You make this mistake and your work is D.O.A… 100% Guaranteed!

I would refer back to the one example I can provide, *The Matrix* trilogy, which I detailed in the Three Act Structure chapter. Though the trilogy is three films, rather than one, the confusion instigated by Neo engaging a different conflict in the third installment as opposed to what's initiated in the original is what killed that franchise. The core conflict of *Star Wars* may have been about the Death Star, but the larger issue was that of the Rebellion against the Empire; and in *Return of the Jedi*, you'll note that the Climax is the resolution of that struggle.

Can you picture that instead of Luke facing Vader and defeating the Emperor, he inexplicably went back to Tatooine, battled sand people, and the rebellion was still fighting for survival at the end? You'd feel cheated and George Lucas would have a much smaller bank account.

Don't Trick Me – Entertain Me!

Most resolutions won't be a surprise to your audience, nor do they need to be. Many novice and advanced screenwriters alike kill themselves trying to outsmart the audience with clever twists and turns. A great twist can be fantastic if it's organic and natural to the story and genre. The trick with most scripts isn't avoiding predictability, it's embracing it, yet finding a creative and original way to show us what we already know is coming.

Let me be crystal clear. I am not suggesting that you make no effort to surprise your audience, but writers must learn that twists and turns don't necessarily belong in all types of films (depending on their genre and tone) and that a film can be predictable and still possess a number of surprises.

I know James Bond is going to come out on top at the end of EVERY single Bond film, but that doesn't preclude the writers from being creative in how that conclusion is reached. The degree to which they are successful has a tremendous impact on whether they wind up with *Skyfall* or *The Living Daylights*.

Is it surprising when Superman is victorious or that Ryan Reynolds and Sandra Bullock end up together in *The Proposal? Slumdog Millionaire* is a great Best Picture winner; did you really think Jamal wouldn't be with Latika in the end?

How about *Miracle* or *Apollo 13?* Both are based on true stories and both have endings the audience is fully aware are coming. Despite that, they're extremely entertaining films. Everyone knew the Titanic would sink and yet the film found a way to both engage and entertain.

The very important lesson is that a movie can be predictable AND enjoyable, as well as surprising and audacious. Such is the case with *Silence of the Lambs*, for example. Did anyone doubt that Clarice would stop Buffalo Bill?

Your challenge, in most cases, is to entertain, not trick the audience. Obviously in a film like *The Sting* or *The Sixth Sense*, that may change, but most films are predictable and that shouldn't be feared. Instead, concoct how to get Mom and Dad to make up or the cop to catch the killer in a fresh way people haven't seen before. That's how you both surprise and entertain an audience. Get creative with location, weather, humor, charm, etc.... It's the process that often requires ingenuity, not the result.

THE NOT HOLLYWOOD ENDING

Most films end on a positive note. This is logical as people are far more likely to be entertained by happy endings than sad ones. Sometimes, however, a film and script are far more compelling when you offer an alternative. Maybe the good guy doesn't win. Perhaps love doesn't prevail or someone integral, including perhaps the protagonist, dies or is killed.

Straight-up tragedy tends, for obvious reasons, to feature in Dramas with life and death stakes, disease, despair, and so forth. You should be aware that movies such as *Terms of Endearment*, *Leaving Las Vegas*, and *Sophie's Choice* are rare and extremely difficult to market. As a result, any screenwriter who isn't already established in the industry will have an exceptionally hard time finding a buyer for this type of work. Not impossible, but very hard. Moreover, movies like this are perhaps the most difficult of all to execute well. The writing has to be near perfect. It requires subtlety and a richness of character that typically only comes with experience. So screenwriter beware...

Films like *Gladiator*, *Braveheart*, *Ghost*, and *Castaway* have what I would term bittersweet endings. In each, sadness permeates the Climax, but the endings are not necessarily tragic or depressing and while all four of these films are considered Dramas, the scope and breadth of their stories allows for success to be mixed with sadness. This concoction combines to deliver bittersweet.

Maximus dies, but gets his revenge; the Scots achieve victory over England despite the execution of William Wallace; Patrick Swayze is dead, but Demi can say goodbye before he's off to heaven; and Tom Hanks accepts the loss of his true love, but marches optimistically into an uncertain future. In such cases, you get to have your cake and eat it too in the form of a positive resolution complemented by the more realistic, not-everything-works-out-perfectly conclusion.

The caveat is it's certainly okay to deviate from the Hollywood, happy ending, but don't do it just for the sake of it. Don't do it because you somehow feel it's more artistic that way or less conventional. This type of Climax is very worthy of your consideration if your story supports it and the resulting emotional response is a positive addition to your work.

THE BIG REVEAL

This is a common addition to a Climax that provides the audience a shocking revelation. "Luke, I am your father!" from *The Empire Strikes Back*, the bulletin board in *The Usual Suspects*, and Bruce Willis being dead in *The Sixth Sense* are notable examples. It may be a reveal that the audience is already aware of, but one or more of the characters are not, such as the unmasking of a superhero to reveal their true identity.

Simply put, the Big Reveal, when it's a true surprise to the audience, is a method to employ that not only leaves people engaged, but often surprised and talking as they exit the film or finish reading your script. Additionally, it is this type of dynamic revelation that has the potential to elevate a movie at a critical moment. If the Climax is in fact 50% of your grade, consider the Big Reveal extra credit that just might take you from a B+ to an A.

Many screenwriters make the mistake of trying to force a Big Reveal because when they work, they REALLY work, but recognize how rare that is. How many truly surprising and special reveals can you recall from films? To an extent, they are genre specific, typically appearing in Thrillers or films with a significant mystery or suspense element. That's not a rule, but certainly worth noting.

Additionally, I would offer that twists like this are extraordinarily difficult to create and implement later in the process. You will be in far better shape if your potential twist is integral to the plot such as in *The Sixth Sense* or *The Usual Suspects*; and in all cases, you prepare from page 1 on so that you can build to its eventual reveal. That is, if you want it to be highly successful.

Yet another reason to outline before you start writing!

The lesson, as it is for many other things in this text, is to employ a Big Reveal when, and only if, it makes sense for your particular story. Otherwise, you're forcing a square peg into a round hole.

KEYS TO REMEMBER

- If you've managed to seduce a reader into sticking with your script until the end, recognize that failing in the Climax to deliver on their hopes for a satisfying conclusion can dramatically lower their overall impression of the work. We remember what's fresh in our minds and if that's disappointment, it won't matter how good the preceding 80 to 100 pages were.

- Many if not most movie climaxes are predictable as far as the who and what. Don't fear that, but make sure to be original when it comes to the how. We know Superman will emerge victorious. Be creative with the finale and thus ensure getting there was worth the journey.

- Make sure the Climax is a direct confrontation between your protagonist and antagonist. There's a reason Darth Vader, not a random stormtrooper, is in the TIE fighter behind Luke Skywalker at the end of *Star Wars*. It is a major failing when screenwriters relegate the antagonist to a minor or insignificant role in the conclusion. They are the cause of the conflict and must be directly involved with its ultimate resolution.

- Regardless of whether the protagonist is successful in resolving the core conflict, make sure the culmination of that journey is either the highest of highs or the lowest of lows. Satisfy your audience with great drama and genuine emotion, no matter the genre.

- Surprising twists and reveals can be superb additions to any script when they are effective and unpredictable. Alternatively, they are often obvious and forced, which has the opposite effect. Make sure it fits your story, and more importantly that it is an unexpected and provocative value add; otherwise you are doing yourself and the script a disservice by forcing its inclusion.

- Your Climax and First Act Break MUST match. This is an unbreakable rule. To do so will leave you with a script that doesn't make any sense and with no hope of realizing your screenwriting dreams.

WRITING EXERCISE: CHASING & RACING

This exercise is designed to assist you in a few vital areas. First, it will hopefully force you to consider alternatives when writing your Climax, as your first idea will rarely be your best. Additionally, the chasing and racing component will assure, regardless of genre, that you write with a deliberate pace, which is critical for any scene or sequence that is supposed to be the ultimate confrontation of forces within a given story. Finally, it requires that you include the antagonist, forcing you as the writer to practice working on making them a worthy opponent and finishing strong with a Climax that will leave your audience with a positive impression.

You are going to write 3 different scenes. The protagonist should once again be your real-life best friend OR the protagonist you wrote your character bio for. In either case, you should know this individual pretty well. For the antagonist, that should either be your planned character from your currently gestating idea, OR choose from the following list:

1. The Joker
2. A Mad Scientist
3. Norman Bates
4. A Lion, a Tiger, or a Bear
5. Your Least Favorite Person
6. Evil Stepmother
7. Your High School Bully/Nemesis
8. Space Pirate
9. Dracula
10. Your Current or Former Boss

In each of the 3 scenes, the characters will be Chasing or Racing. One could be chasing the other or they could be racing against the clock to get somewhere prior to an event, such as an explosion or a murder.

In each scene, change the modes of transport AND the genre.

A comedy might have a blimp race with a Mad Scientist. Another might be a Fantasy where a lost Crusader battles Vlad the Impaler (the original Dracula!) in ancient Romania while a final version could be an intergalactic battle with a cyborg Blackbeard to protect the legendary Queen of Xilox. It could also be your friend racing to catch a train before the love of their life speeds away with your boss. Switch it up and try different things. Remember, the first idea or instinct isn't necessarily the best you can come up with.

Enjoy the ride!

CHAPTER 8

Dialogue...
Distinct Voice Means Not Your Own

The most important thing about dialogue is not to write all the characters in your voice and to differentiate each character from one another. This is called **Distinct Voice** and it is one of the final barriers between amateur and professional-grade screenwriting. The natural tendency for all screenwriters, and certainly more so for inexperienced ones, is to ask themselves before each bit of dialogue, "What would I say here?" It may not be a conscious act, but it is nevertheless our natural instinct. As a result of this, the dialogue all sounds the same; worse still, it all sounds like you.

People sound very different from one another. Our experiences and backgrounds ensure that. Male, female, old, young, gay, straight, educated, naïve, arrogant, sarcastic, southern, Portuguese, white, black, born-again Christian, liberal, etc.... Not only does an eighty-year-old Asian grandmother, born in Okinawa and now living in Baton Rouge, sound different from an eleven-year-old boy in Seattle... **neither is likely to sound anything like you!**

This is why character bios or at the very least an abbreviated facsimile of one are so important. Do any of these folks look like they would sound alike?

Before you start writing dialogue for a character, even a minor one, take five minutes and ask yourself: Who are they? How old are they? Where are they from? Are they educated? Do they have any quirks like constantly saying "you know" or "like" between statements? Do they tend to interrupt others? Do they overuse big words or slur their speech? Are they argumentative, serious, sarcastic, romantic? How long do you suppose it would take to answer these few questions? Imagine the difference in your dialogue if you have those answers BEFORE you start writing.

Ask these questions and others to provide a basic sense of their speech patterns and what they sound like. You want to avoid monotone, droning dialogue that puts the audience to sleep, unless it's on purpose such as Ben Stein's teacher in *Ferris Bueller's Day Off*. That role is iconic because instead of just being a random teacher, John Hughes made him quirky and memorable. Did he write a bio for the teacher? I seriously doubt it, but I can pretty much guarantee that at some point, he stopped and asked himself how this character could sound unique and not simply be a normal, average teacher calling attendance.

Remember that speech and dialogue have a rhythm. People don't talk in complete sentences. There are interruptions, pauses to think about what we want to say, slang, sneezing, etc.... People can be passive or argumentative and this will reflect in their dialogue. People can be poetic or speak with alliteration. They can be repetitive or constantly mumble. Consider all of this when writing dialogue and crafting Distinct Voice for your characters.

THE ECONOMY OF LANGUAGE

In general, don't say more than you need to in order to make a point, answer a question, or disseminate information. The exception would be if it were natural for the specific character that is speaking to say more than is necessary. Otherwise, allow for the actor to breathe life into the words via their performance and recognize that as a visual medium, the audience will have the added benefit of body language, facial expressions, and other visual cues to augment your words.

The next time you are with a group of people, be a fly on the wall and take a couple of minutes and don't talk... Just stand back and listen to how they sound and watch how much is communicated via nonverbal methods.

Some things to consider: Replace "yes" and "no" with gestures or shrugs. Eliminate the first words in your dialogue such as "Well" or "I mean" or "You see" as they are often unnecessary. Don't overuse the character's name. This is a funny quirk for some screenwriters who seem to forget about the giant screen an audience will be looking at. You don't need to remind us whom a character is speaking to. We can see them so don't say "Adam, where are you?" and "Adam, what time is it?" Just "What time is it?" This is one of those errors that frequently shows up; when it does, it's obvious and annoying, but it's also an easy fix. People don't speak that way so try and avoid it.

Another helpful tip is that you should look to enter scenes late and leave them early. We don't always need to see the greetings, salutations, and small talk that occur between characters prior to saying the stuff that actually matters to a film's plot. Similarly, we don't need to see the goodbyes that take place before a scene concludes. I can't begin to tell you how common this is and how many pages are wasted at the beginning and end of scenes.

As an example, a couple goes to dinner at another couple's house. Instead of transitioning from the preceding scene to them already sitting at the dinner table and deep into the relevant conversation, pages and pages are included of the arrival, taking the coats, and inane small talk until FINALLY, we get to the important stuff. All of the helloes and goodbyes can amount to several wasted pages! Think about how a reader feels wading through such nonsense.

It will save a lot of time and help the pacing considerably if you enter a scene with the characters already settled and talking and/or cut away from a scene when the necessary information is conveyed and all that remains is a goodbye that the audience doesn't need to see. It is necessary to show arrivals and departures at certain times for the plot of your film, but in general, most scenes not only don't require it, but are better for not including it, so be mindful of this.

SPEECH FORM

All useful information need not be delivered via standard, pleasant conversation. Consider alternatives whenever possible. Perhaps it might be more arresting to impart important details via an argument or have one character eavesdrop on another or maybe by utilizing an anecdote. Sometimes, typical conversation is not only less stimulating, but also easily replaced by something more engaging. Don't forget the point made in the Character chapter about conflict being interesting. Arguments are not only more compelling to watch than standard conversation, they are far more likely to elicit provocative or even uncomfortable revelations that are more likely to advance your story.

Let's say you have a scene with three couples playing charades. One of the couples is angry at one another. You have two choices, the first of which is for one of the characters to just start sniping about why they're pissed, and the other option is to have one of them passive aggressively use the game to draw a picture that conveys their anger silently, amidst the uncomfortable gaze of the others. Which sounds more engaging to watch on a screen?

The Usual Suspects is an Oscar-winning screenplay that is a perfect example of this. Kevin Spacey's character could have just explained things in a straightforward manner to Chazz Palminteri's Customs Agent, but instead, the screenwriter chose to infuse that film with one great anecdote after another. As an example, rather than simply saying Kaiser Söze was an evil badass, he tells a story about how Söze came home to find his wife raped and his children brutalized by a rival gang. Rather than cooperate, he kills his own family and all but one of their attackers so that he can go forth and tell everyone what happens to those who mess with Keyser Söze. Now he's the boogeyman.

His actions make him a myth, an evil legend to the criminal underworld. It's a great beat in the story and infinitely more captivating than just saying he's evil or diabolical or whatever other adjective wouldn't come close to achieving the same level of characterization.

As another, much more grandiose example, Musicals do more than simply turn dialogue into song, they are the catalyst for extreme emotion, providing added insight into the characters. Musicals inspire passion while relaying relevant information. Think about "Somewhere Over the Rainbow" in *The Wizard of Oz*, "Circle of Life" in *The Lion King*, or "Summer Nights" in *Grease*. Baz Luhrmann's *Moulin Rouge* utilized "Come What May" as a secret method for Christian and Satine to profess their love for one another without overtly saying the words.

The Adam Sandler Dramedy *Funny People* included standup comedy routines where the fear and turmoil of the cancer-stricken character is evident via his extremely dark attempts at comedy. He could have simply told his buddies he was scared or angry, but allowing his emotional conflict to appear in his shtick is far more compelling.

The bottom line is you need to consider alternative methods of making important points in your story rather than just saying everything in black and white through standard character exposition. That will get boring and demonstrate a tremendous lack of creativity on your part.

SUBTEXT

From dictionary.com:
1. *The underlying or implicit meaning, as of a literary work.*

From Wikipedia:
1. *Any content of a creative work which is not announced explicitly by the characters or author, but is implicit or becomes something understood by the observer of the work as the production unfolds.*
2. *The unspoken thoughts and motives of characters — what they really think and believe.*
3. *A frequently used method of subtly inserting social or political commentary into fiction.*

The use (and more importantly, the mastery) of subtext is one of the more advanced tools in a screenwriter's arsenal. When you are able to say more than what is explicitly revealed in your dialogue, you will have graduated to a higher level of writing that is ultimately vital to anyone interested in earning a living as a professional screenwriter.

Often, it is relatively simple and innocuous, obvious to audiences who are easily able to read between the lines. Here's a very simple, hypothetical example:

```
Lisa stomps upstairs, blowing right past her
stunned parents, sitting in the living room. They
hear her bedroom door slam. Diane rises and heads
up to check on her daughter.

She knocks on Lisa's bedroom door.

                    DIANE
          Honey, are you okay?

                    LISA
          FINE!
```

What's more interesting, Lisa's angry response that clearly holds information back or if she were to immediately say everything that is bothering her including the who, what, where, and when?

Here's another example, this one from *The Italian Job*. Note the final line and how much more it suggests about Bridger and his relationship with his daughter.

```
JOHN BRIDGER, 50s, is a tasteful man buying a very tasteful,
and very expensive, diamond necklace. The saleswoman wraps it
up as he dials a number on his cell phone.
                    STELLA (V.O.)
          Hello?

                    JOHN BRIDGER
          Hi, sweetie.

INT. STELLA'S CONDO - PHILADELPHIA - INTERCUT

STELLA BRIDGER, 27, crushingly attractive, has just stepped out
of the shower, hair still wet, body wrapped in a towel.
                    STELLA
          Daddy. How are you?

                    JOHN BRIDGER
          I'm sending you something.

                    STELLA
          Really? Does it smell nice?

                    JOHN BRIDGER
          No. But it's sparkly.

                    STELLA
          Does it come with a receipt?
```

Beyond the simplicity of hidden meaning and implied thoughts or actions buried behind bits of dialogue are a variety of additional methods by which subtext can be conveyed.

For example, the use of METAPHOR is quite common. Several movies have used fireworks or other similar effects as a metaphor to suggest sex without showing it. Such was the case in both *To Catch a Thief* and *The Naked Gun*, two very different films.

In *The Shawshank Redemption*, Andy locks himself in the warden's office and plays a piece of classical music that serves for him and many of the men who hear it over the PA system as a metaphor for freedom. It transports them outside the walls of the prison. Music is one of the more common uses of metaphor in film with songs creating an attitude or conveying emotion.

In *The Last Samurai*, just before facing a hopeless climactic battle, Cruise's Captain Algren talks to Ken Watanabe's Katsumoto about the battle of Thermopylae to break through the language barrier and suggest the value of honor, even in the face of certain death. He uses a historical ANECDOTE to far more elegantly convey his message rather than stating emphatically that the odds are not in their favor. Later, just prior to the commencement of the battle, the following exchange takes place:

```
     Algren stands with Katsumoto and Ujio. Graham is
     there, too. The silent Samurai stands near Algren,
     as always. They peer into the plain beyond at an
     awe-inspiring sight. Katsumoto's 500 samurai face
     a staggering 5,000 soldiers.

                    KATSUMOTO
          What happened to those three
          hundred warriors at Thermopylae?

                    ALGREN
                 (a grim smile)
          Dead to the last man.

     Katsumoto glances at him, smiles.
```

Take note of the last line. Katsumoto smiles at the revelation that every Spartan was killed. Does he not understand? Of course he does. He's pleased because he does understand as the subtext is about honor, which to him, is more important than life.

In some cases, such as in the jail scene in *The Dark Knight*, SILENCE or the very lack of any dialogue is often more effective than any words you might write. In that scene, the absence of commentary from the Joker was far more unsettling than a bunch of threats or heavy handed dialogue would have been.

INNUENDO, which can simply be an extension of metaphor in some cases, is also an effective option. In *Gone in 60 Seconds*, Nic Cage and Angelina Jolie are sitting in a car, waiting. With a sudden stretch of time alone and nothing to do, the talk turns to car parts, but sex is clearly the real topic of conversation.

Get into the habit of looking beyond the obvious nature of most straightforward dialogue and try to recognize opportunities to use subtext to provide a more nuanced and ultimately more professional screenplay.

Great dialogue takes practice. This should not come as any kind of surprise, but it isn't simply about practicing phrasing or learning to be witty and succinct. You must get into the habit of thinking outside the box. How, other than simple dialogue, can a point be made? Information can't always come easily, nor should it often come directly. Sometimes the best dialogue is none at all and that is a very difficult, yet important lesson to learn.

KEYS TO REMEMBER

- Remove your voice from the dialogue process. You are not a character in the story so none of the characters should sound like you. It is a frequent mistake that screenwriters make having all the characters sound the same, and typically that shared voice is the writer's.

- DO NOT ask yourself as you write dialogue, "What would I say here?"
- Since it is often done unconsciously, force yourself to consider, "What would John or Jane say here?"
- Bios, even quick, 5-minute ones will dramatically help you to achieve distinct voice, so don't be lazy!
- More often than not, less is more. People tend not to speak in long speeches. Often a gesture or sound can and should replace words. Consider all your options because frequently, there's a simpler and more natural way to convey whatever dialogue or message you are working on.
- Don't always have characters speak pleasantly with one another. Heightened emotions can lead to more dynamic revelations and more interesting conversations.
- Novice screenwriters tend to be very literal and conspicuous in their writing, failing to use any subtext or nuance when making a point. The inclusion of such subtleties is one of the more obvious indicators of actual screenwriting talent.
- Obvious is boring. Use things like metaphor, innuendo, anecdotes, or even silence to craft a more sophisticated piece of work.

WRITING EXERCISE: TRAPPED IN AN ELEVATOR

In this exercise, the objective is to utilize Distinct Voice as you fashion three unique and markedly different individuals. Work to capture the essence of how each one sounds when they talk and the methods, other than normal speech, that they also employ.

Who are three strangers you met or interacted with recently? Perhaps...

- A waiter at a restaurant
- A new employee at work
- A blind date from last weekend
- A friend of your sibling or spouse
- The mechanic who's fixing your car
- A new hairdresser

It will help if you include at least one male and one female, as you will then be forced to write the opposite gender as well, something that will certainly be necessary in your screenwriting. Variation in their ages is also helpful.

The three characters will, not surprisingly, be trapped in an elevator.

Write a scene that features all three, but challenge yourself to use Distinct Voice. Make them sound different from one another and nothing like you.

The genre and circumstances are both at your discretion. Maybe it's a Thriller and one of the characters is claustrophobic. It could be a Romantic Comedy and two of the characters are having a meet cute while the third is forced to watch uncomfortably. It could be an Action movie and they get stuck in the middle of an earthquake. It's entirely up to you.

Do short bios for the characters to aid your efforts. You shouldn't need more than a few minutes for each. Just give yourself the basics to provide a sense of their voice. Where are they from? What is their education, family background, etc.? Why are they in the elevator? Where are they going? What is their state of mind? Are they having a good or bad day? Work to write 3 characters, each with an obvious and recognizable voice of their own.

BONUS WRITING EXERCISE:
READ BETWEEN THE LINES

This exercise is intended to aid in your ability to create subtext in your writing.

You are going to write 3 scenes, each with 2 characters.

In each of the scenes, try to keep the conversations relatively innocuous, while at the same time suggesting underlying intent, hidden messages, and ulterior motives from one or both characters.

1. In the first scenario, a teenage boy or girl is visiting their father for the first time in prison.
2. In the second scenario, a divorced husband and wife who haven't seen one another in five years find themselves randomly seated next to each other on a full airplane.
3. In the third scenario, the male or female victim of a violent crime is visited by the mother of the perpetrator.

How will you convey the emotions of the scene without the characters just stating everything they are thinking and feeling?

What will be evident between the lines and obvious in the silence?

Can you make the reader understand what they're experiencing and perhaps even wanting to say, but not?

This can be a highly effective exercise when it comes to learning how to better incorporate subtext into your work. I highly recommend you take advantage of this opportunity to learn and practice. Your writing will greatly benefit as a result.

CHAPTER 9

Concept...
Get Off to a Great Start

Attempting to define what makes a good concept is not dissimilar from trying to explain what good taste or a great sense of humor is. Everyone thinks they've got it and therein lies the challenge ... How does one explain it without simply saying they know it when they hear it?

Please keep in mind as you review this section that the information is geared towards spec screenwriting and (to narrow it even further) to primarily new and aspiring screenwriters that have yet to secure steady industry work or an agent. This is important because it means whatever concept you devise and then execute must be a lot more than just well written ... Its first mission must be to get you industry attention, competition accolades, and/or representation, which makes commercial viability another vital element for you to consider.

Many concepts fall into a category I would dub as "execution dependent." This isn't a place you want to be, particularly for a first or early effort. Most notably because concepts such as these require a level of expertise rarely on display from the most talented of writers, let alone novices. They need a writer with tremendous talent, often stemming from experience, who is capable of executing a difficult, dramatic script with rich characters and controversial themes and subject matter.

Execution-dependent material also usually lacks a big creative and commercial hook, relying more on character than plot. It frequently demands that a writer handle controversial subjects, such as religion, unconventional sexual appetites, the afterlife, homosexuality, racism, anti-American sentiment, and other taboo topics that are incredibly challenging to get right. A final element would be ideas that require A-list talent to produce because without such box office draws, films such as these rarely are able to find an audience. Setting aside independently produced films, studios won't tread in these waters without the security of big names that they can use to market the film. If they can't sell explosions, sex, blood, and/or comedy, they typically demand star power.

Many people have an interest in screenwriting because there is a passion project they are desperate to write. In a vast number of these cases, it's a true story, often about a family member. Setting aside the fact that rarely will any novice writer do justice to these stories in their first script, these ideas are always a red flag. **Professional screenwriters don't have one story to tell, they have dozens**.

Screenwriters will also, quite often, move to emulate the work of some of their favorite filmmakers. This holds true with decisions on concept as well.

Recognize that such filmmakers have years of experience and have earned the right to work in more complicated arenas. They don't face the same challenges you will in terms of securing representation or selling the material. What is a good concept for Quentin Tarantino, Christopher Nolan, Woody Allen, or any well-established writer/ director is quite possibly not so for you.

Perhaps the most important consideration when determining the concept of your script is what your hopes or intentions are for the project. If you are a working screenwriter, then simply put, you're looking to sell it and make a movie. You likely have the representation to make that a reality and the talent to deliver. This affords you a great deal of freedom when making such a decision.

Alternatively, if you are new to screenwriting, practice and experience may be your priority. If you've written a few scripts and are looking to take the next step, maybe your goal is to submit to competitions or to use it to secure representation. All of these should influence the type of concept you choose, or at the very least, the type(s) to avoid.

For example, if you are looking for representation, execution dependent is not going to be a good choice for you. Agents are interested in high concept, commercial material that they can sell. Conversely, if competitions are your goal, Drama may be the ticket, though competitions cater to all genres. I will reiterate, however, that Drama is the hardest genre to write well and the epitome of execution dependent. You might want to seriously consider saving that until your talent is at a level where you can deliver a strong result.

There are many definitions for the term High Concept. Most seem to suggest it's about being able to pitch the idea in one sentence. The problem with that is I could describe a film as "One man self destructs and tears his family apart thanks to a ceaseless addiction to gambling." That's one sentence, but it definitely isn't high concept. Though simplicity and brevity are vital components, there are two key additional elements required for an idea to be high concept.

The first is a fresh, creative hook. Most themes, motivations, and plots have been done, sometimes well and often not. There are only so many reasons why one person harms another, why people fall in love, why a crime is committed, and so on. Your mission is to be original within the confines of often predictable and formulaic situations.

The best examples of this are always the simplest because they're easy to visualize. Such as using the *Die Hard* formula on a bus with the simple caveat that it can't drop below 50 mph without blowing up. Another might be doing a movie about a guy trying to lose his virginity; certainly not a new idea except this guy is 40 years old. Serial killer films are common, but how about one that uses the 7 deadly sins to frame his murders?

I hear pitches for *Speed*, *The 40-Year-Old Virgin*, or *Se7en* and I know those are great high concepts, even without the box office numbers to prove it.

It's extremely rare, but occasionally a screenwriter devises something entirely refreshing and unique. *The Truman Show*, *Pleasantville*, *Being John Malkovich*, and *Groundhog Day* exemplify this exceedingly rare circumstance. If you are fortunate enough to conceive a truly original idea, congratulations on catching lightning in a bottle and prepare for others to copy your efforts for years to come.

Who you gonna call?

The second element is mass appeal. High concept films have large audiences. They fill multiplexes during the summer and at Christmas. They attract the top moviegoing audiences of young men and teenagers. High concept ideas tend to possess very simple yet enticing hooks, thereby giving them a broader audience. They don't tackle hot-button issues, alienate people based on sensitive subject matter, or appear overly highbrow or cerebral to suggest an opinion, point of view, or message beyond pure entertainment value.

So what are some of the factors that might help you devise a compelling, and attractive, high concept idea?

Here are a few …

- Fish-out-of-water stories … *Beverly Hills Cop* or *Sister Act*
- Tapping into prominent fears or phobias … *Snakes on a Plane* or *Saw*
- Pop culture appeal … *The Fast and the Furious*, *Blue Crush*, or *Rounders*
- Location … *Night at the Museum* or *Paul Blart: Mall Cop*
- Twists on familiar or existing formulas … *XXX* or *Underworld*

- Holiday Tie-ins ... *Independence Day, Four Christmases, New Year's Eve*
- Themes or situations audiences can relate to ... *Fatal Attraction, Taken, What Women Want,* or *Guess Who's Coming to Dinner*
- Alternative tone or setting to previously seen material ... *Disturbia, Clueless, 10 Things I Hate About You,* or *The Magnificent Seven*

Another concept that has been done a number of times is one in which a kid or kids must step up to save the day, generally outwitting or defeating one or more adults in the process. This was probably best accomplished in *Home Alone,* though many others have tread in that territory.

Disaster movies can be a fruitful topic. Some have been extremely successful, such as *Armageddon, Twister,* and *The Day After Tomorrow* while others largely failed to inspire audiences, such as *Volcano, Daylight, Hard Rain,* or *Firestorm.*

Body-switching setups have yielded everything from *Face/Off* and *Big* (very successful) to *17 Again* and *The Hot Chick* (not so much). Wish fulfillment is also quite common. Some are literally about wishes being granted such as *13 Going on 30, Freaky Friday,* or the previously mentioned *Big.* Others tap into common or popular wishes such as modern fairy tales like *Pretty Woman* and *The Princess Diaries.* Some are what I term *glimpses.* They offer a character a chance to see what if ... *The Family Man* and *It's a Wonderful Life,* for example.

This section is meant to help in the creation of strong concepts for spec screenplays so adaptations and remakes would not be advisable. The likelihood is that you are not in a position due to money or credibility to secure the underlying rights to the material you wish to adapt and you should ALWAYS own your own work.

The one exception would be a new interpretation of public domain material such as *Cruel Intentions* from *Dangerous Liaisons, Clueless* from *Emma,* or simply doing a new version of material such as *Robin Hood, Romeo & Juliet, Cinderella,* or *The Count of Monte Cristo.*

When all is said and done, great high concepts are obvious by the fact that after hearing one line, you want to see the movie or at the very least, understand why many others would. That's why Hollywood loves them. They're easy to sell and appeal to a vast audience. For those hoping to break into the industry, you should also note that high concept ideas are far more likely to get you read by agents and managers because it's much easier to entice them with a short, succinct pitch, either verbally or in writing. A great idea can not only sell itself, it can camouflage flaws in a script while execution-dependent work hides nothing and leaves it entirely up to the quality of writing.

THEME

You'll often read interviews where actors and directors state that it was the theme and journey of the characters that drew them to a particular script, as opposed to the concept. Frankly, these two things go hand in hand, but it is crucial that you give considerable thought to what the theme or themes of your story are. In development circles, you'll often hear talk of a script's connective tissue or the *thru line*. What's really being discussed is the heart of the story.

Take *Titanic* and *The Social Network* for example. Both are based on true events, but are dramatized for entertainment value. In both cases, the screenwriters needed to find a personal connection to engage the audience's interest because they already knew the final outcomes. In the case of *Titanic*, James Cameron fashioned an epic love story and then took it a step further by making it a class struggle as well. With *The Social Network*, Aaron Sorkin boiled down Zuckerberg's motives for launching one of the greatest tech companies in history to a desire to "friend" the college girl he desperately wanted forgiveness from. Other themes exist as well, such as the entitled Winklevoss twins versus the nerd from nowhere, Mark's jealously of Eduardo for being tapped by a private club, and Sean Parker's insecurity.

Look at *Forrest Gump*. That is an epic journey, but at its core, the themes are simple. Life, love, friendship, and family. They drive the whole story and all of the various relationships. Everyone remembers "Life is like a box of chocolates ..." but what came before that? "Mama always said" was how that line began.

What will drive your story? What themes will be the beating heart of the concept you work to execute? Carefully consider this question because this is where a film graduates from basic and ordinary to emotional and engaging. If making the audience care about the characters is your top priority, theme is one of your best weapons to achieve that.

KEYS TO REMEMBER

- For anyone who is just starting out and not yet established within the industry, bear in mind that commercial viability must be a major consideration when devising your concept. Without it, you are far less likely to secure anyone's interest in even reading the material, let alone pursuing it as a buyer.

- If you aren't ready or talented enough to hit a home run on an execution-dependent idea, go high concept and don't look back.

- Depending on your goals and intentions for the script, give careful consideration to any elements that will offend or alienate and thereby diminish your prospects. Sometimes controversy and taboo subject matter can be provocative and other times it is simply a deterrent. You must learn to identify which applies in your case.

- Those of you who are investigating screenwriting because you have a single passion project you are determined to write, consider that rarely, if ever, will a novice screenwriter do justice to such a story as their first and only script, particularly because most of these projects tend to be execution-dependent dramas.

- Before settling on a concept, consider what your goals and/ or intentions are for the material and then try and find the best possible concept to help you achieve those objectives. If you hope to sell the script, you better make sure it's something millions of people would pay to see. Just because a story means the world to you doesn't mean random folks in Baltimore, Barcelona, and Beijing will feel the same.

- High Concept requires more than the ability to pitch the story in one line. It must include a fresh and creative hook along with mass audience appeal.

- Don't forget to give your concept a beating heart. A clever idea or hook is great, but for a reader or audience to truly engage and care about the story, it must possess an emotional core to drive the characters and story. Motives matter!

WRITING EXERCISE:
INVITATION TO INSPIRATION

If you don't already have an idea for a script or movie, the following exercise might inspire something. If you do, perhaps it gives you something better or maybe it just helps you figure out what you'll do after you finish your current project. At the very least, it might spark some ideas for scenes to be included in a current or future effort.

Begin by writing 10 What If's ...
WHAT IF a new plague broke out in Europe?
WHAT IF treasure was buried under your ex-mother-in-law's house?
WHAT IF the assassination of JFK failed?
WHAT IF you fell in love with your best friend's parent or child?
WHAT IF a tsunami hit Los Angeles?

That's 5 pretty generic ones, but you get the idea.

Next, write down 10 locations you think would be great settings for a film.

The Summer Olympics	The Mall of America
Carnival in Rio	Angkor Wat
The Burning Man Festival	The Amazon Rainforest
Easter Island	Prohibition-Era Chicago
The Orient Express in the 1960s	The Panama Canal

Now make a list of the 10 most interesting, disgusting, comical, or bizarre jobs you can think of or find. I did an online search for "bizarre jobs" and found these:

La-Z-Boy Furniture Tester	Amusement Park Vomit Collector
Weed Farmer	Dice Inspector
Professional Whistler	Armpit Sniffer
Golf Ball Diver	Professional Sleeper
Pet Food Taster	Snake Milker

Finally, make a list of 10 motives for murder, 10 excuses for forgetting an anniversary, and 10 reasons to fly to another country tonight. After all this, you should have the beginnings of some pretty intriguing ideas spanning many different genres.

BONUS WRITING EXERCISE:
LET THE MUSIC MOVE YOU

This is a second exercise designed to help give you ideas, but more importantly, to force you to be creative in your thinking with regards to concept.

Begin by picking a song.

It can be anything. A current hit, a classic tune, old school R&B … whatever sparks your interest; however, I wouldn't recommend classical as the titles won't be particularly conducive to this exercise.

Use the title as the basis for 5 new movie concepts.

As an example, take the Eric Clapton song "After Midnight." Maybe it's the title of a Romantic Comedy that unfolds during the graveyard shift at a casino in Lake Tahoe.

Alternatively, it could be a Thriller about a twisted married couple who ambush and murder police officers at 12:02 am on Tuesday nights.

Perhaps it's a Drama about a seemingly conservative and very composed female surgeon, who as it turns out, is hiding a very dysfunctional nightlife.

It could be a Comedy set in Barney's Laugh Factory, a nightlife fixture in Kodiak, Alaska, or maybe it's a Science Fiction film about alien abductions that occur just after midnight from every world city that begins with the letter Z.

Your concepts should include plot points and as much detail as you can muster. Have some fun with it and see what you come up with. You never know, it might just lead to something you actually want to write.

CHAPTER 10

How to Begin a Scene...

Seven Vital Questions

With experience, many of the steps one takes to write an effective and compelling scene become instinctive, driven by your subconscious and a lot of practice. It's like driving a car. Remember when you first got your license, how nervous you were getting on the freeway or parallel parking? Now you just do it, generally without much thought and perhaps even while talking on the phone or eating ice cream. This doesn't happen until you're several *scripts* (not scenes) in. So the question is, how do you write a scene? What should your initial approach be? What follows are SEVEN VITAL QUESTIONS that will substantially help you craft effective scenes that include everything they must to engage and entertain.

QUESTION #1: **What needs to happen in the scene?**

Some books suggest you determine what the needs of the character(s) are, but I disagree or I should say, that's only half the battle. People tend to avoid conflict unless pressed to face it. Plot, regardless of genre, is driven by drama, and drama requires conflict. Your First Act Break establishes a core conflict for your film and your Climax resolves it. In between, your protagonist and other characters move through the story either to help resolve the conflict or prevent its resolution, sometimes directly and in other cases peripherally, depending on the significance of each character to the story. In either case, smaller conflicts arise along the way that must be addressed to reach the conclusion. So what needs to happen?

At the First Act Break of *Die Hard*, terrorists take over Nakatomi Plaza, but a shoeless John McClane escapes. So what **must** come next? In that case, his first instinct is to get someplace safe and call for help. How is that best achieved? The decision that was made was to have him pull a fire alarm. In *The Proposal*, Ryan Reynolds and Sandra Bullock arrive in Alaska. If you are the screenwriter, what must follow? An introduction to the family is required, but finding a surprise party makes the reveal of the engagement ten times as awkward.

In both of these cases, as in any screenplay, there are always options, perhaps not what must come next, but always how it might be approached and/or delivered. Perhaps what needs to happen is moving from point A to point B or it could be the discovery and/or reveal of new information. It could be a love scene because they tend to advance character, plot, and the commercial prospects of a film. Maybe it is a fight or confrontation. Regardless, take a moment to ask yourself, based on what you already know about the characters, as well as the plot coming out of the previous scene, what needs to occur next? It is then your responsibility to discern how best to creatively deliver on that.

QUESTION #2: **Who needs to be there and who doesn't?**

Often, writers place characters in scenes when their presence isn't necessary. It wastes a reader's time and adds to potential confusion. Too many characters can be distracting so keep the clutter to a minimum. Make sure everyone present serves a purpose, even if all they do is sit quietly in a corner.

This is a situation where the perception of a reader versus an audience is very different. With a large screen, an audience doesn't need to remember who's present — everyone is visible. Conversely, when it is indicated that many characters are present in a screenplay, the reader is essentially being told they must remember each of them. I cannot stress enough how frustrating it is to read that several characters are present during a scene's setup and then one or more of them have no function or role to play. If you take the time to indicate someone is in a scene, be sure their presence advances the plot in some way.

QUESTION #3: **Where could the scene take place?**

This is huge! The tendency of most writers is to put a scene in the most obvious and therefore least interesting of locations: a bedroom, office, the car, kitchen, etc. The writer gets wrapped up in the importance of the exchange between two characters and never considers that there might be a more interesting setting than the library or the den or the police station. More often than you might think, the same conversation you stick in the kitchen could just as easily take place at the rodeo, in a pawnshop, or at a Ferrari dealership, depending on what makes sense within the confines of your particular story. Such a move tends to elevate the effectiveness of a scene and offer many additional alternatives that wouldn't otherwise be possible sitting in a more staid and conventional location.

Consider the first conversation between George Clooney and Jennifer Lopez in *Out of Sight*. It would have been easy to stick them in the back seat, but putting them in the trunk where every sound and movement has meaning and the limited space forces close contact and intimacy makes that scene memorable and great. In *The Wedding Singer*, the Climax could easily have been at a house or in a backyard, but putting it on an airplane allowed for the separation between first class and coach, the presence of Billy Idol, and an audience for Adam Sandler and Drew Barrymore's proclamations of love for one another.

QUESTION #4: **How long should the scene be?**

This is more important than you might realize as many, many, MANY writers go long with their scripts as has been stated. With a given scene, you may have some great ideas and very well might write 5 fantastic pages, but the more important question is whether the relevant content could have been delivered in a quarter page, or if you even have 5 pages to spare. It's not simply that sometimes less is more; it's also that often, the pages are better spent elsewhere and you must be conscious of that. Prioritize your scenes and determine the proper length.

The Road Map can be extremely helpful with this. It doesn't need to be exact and it certainly can change, but you absolutely should have a relative sense of how important each scene is compared to the others around it. So how much room do you have for a conversation between your main character and his mother, for example? Maybe it's particularly important and worthy of 3 or 4 pages, but if not, perhaps it's only a snippet of a conversation that occupies half a page. Making those determinations, at least generally and before you start, will help avoid the common pitfall of making every scene long, dense, and detailed, regardless of its significance to the story.

QUESTION #5: **What might happen to surprise the audience?**

Often, the genre may inform the answer to this question or at least the tone of the surprise. If your scene is in a bank, does the sudden appearance of a bank robber or the accidental bursting of a dye pack on a careless teller improve it? If your scene is in Central Park, does the addition of a streaker make it funnier? Your protagonist has just picked up her child from school. Does an incident of road rage on the way home provide tension and a chance to offer necessary character depth?

Take the film *Honeymoon in Vegas*. Nicolas Cage is desperately racing to stop Sarah Jessica Parker from marrying the duplicitous James Caan. They are in Vegas and Cage is haphazardly making his way there from Hawaii. Now the easy and obvious Climax would have involved Cage flying to Vegas and racing to the chapel or into the hotel for a big confrontation. Who would have expected him to parachute down to the strip as part of the Flying Elvises, Utah Chapter!

Dressed in illuminated Elvis regalia, he lands to sweep Parker, dressed as a showgirl (you'll have to see it to understand) into his arms. No surprise that they wound up together, but this exemplifies the notion of arriving at key moments in entertaining and unexpected ways. The important issue is that if you never surprise your audience, you are far more likely to bore them.

QUESTION #6: **Is the scene necessary?**

Another overlooked question to ask yourself with regards to scene construction is whether a given scene is even necessary to the progression of your story. Consider what the effect would be if the scene were literally cut from the script. We've all heard of the cutting room floor so we all know scenes can be removed with little or no negative effect and often a very positive one. This begs the question, does the story still make sense if a given scene is deleted? Is anything lost? You'd be surprised at how often the answer is yes to the first and no to the second, but the scene still remains in the script.

Screenwriters get attached to their own ideas and when they think one is a keeper, the notion of cutting it, even if it's the right thing to do, is heretical to even imagine. This isn't about whether a scene is well written or funny or exciting. It may be all or none of those things, but I promise you it will be left on the cutting room floor if it doesn't further the story in even a minor way so save yourself the later frustration.

I wrote and directed a small film entitled *It's Dark Here*, which included a scene where the protagonist climbs to the top of a massive oil tank overlooking the valley where he lives. It's meant to be an emotional moment and as the director, I very much looked forward to what I knew would be a great visual and it was... the character standing on the roof at sunset, gazing across the entire suburban valley. The problem was that it was redundant with an earlier shot that fit better and as a result, it needed to be cut from the film. Scripts and films require hard choices and I promise you, if you're not willing to make them yourself, someone else will certainly step in and do it for you.

QUESTION #7: **What are some options and/or alternatives?**

When devising a scene, particularly an important or pivotal moment in your screenplay, give yourself options. Your first idea may be your best, but let's face it, the odds are against that, especially if you're willing to put in some real time and effort. Regardless, you certainly improve your odds at achieving originality and creativity if after answering all the previous questions, you take an additional stretch of time to devise one, two, maybe even three alternate ways you could execute the scene before you actually begin writing. Take that *Honeymoon In Vegas* example… do you really think that was the first idea for how the Climax would go or is it more likely that it was the 10th and the screenwriter chose not to settle for easy or obvious?

MAKE A LIST!

They're still your ideas, but now you have the ability to pick the best of the bunch, rather than simply settling for what's easy or fast because I promise you, a living as a screenwriter is not likely if you do.

KEYS TO REMEMBER

- Most screenwriters, particularly those with less experience, tend to write in a hurry. They go with their first ideas, skip outlining, ignore character development, and just dive in. Slow down and consider all your options before writing scenes, as it will substantially aid in your ability to look past first or obvious paths and seek out less conventional and far more interesting options.

- Writers often ignore common sense and include scenes or actions that are irrelevant or unnecessary to the progression of plot or character development. It's one of the primary causes of early screenwriting efforts running long.

- Make sure any character you place in a scene has a purpose in being there. Everyone doesn't need dialogue, but they do need a purpose.

- When it comes to picking the location of a scene, some added thought will often lead to far more cinematic and engaging options. Such locations tend also to provide greater opportunities for action, comedy, heightened conflict, and the unexpected.

- You have a finite amount of space to work with and while it seems limitless at the outset, that is rarely the case later on. Determine if a scene warrants multiple pages or whether a few lines or a fraction of page is sufficient to accomplish what is necessary.

- What surprising elements can you introduce in your scenes to upset the status quo? What's more interesting, walking down 5th Avenue uninterrupted or passing a throng of stormtroopers or a rogue elephant?

- Make sure every scene merits inclusion in the final product or you risk a slow pace, confusion, boredom, and most especially, rejection.

- Your first idea about how to execute a scene may ultimately be your best, but you'll never know if you don't take the time to consider other ideas.

WRITING EXERCISE: Act 1, Scene 2

The only scene you can be assured that someone will read when you submit your script is the opening or first scene. Many of those that will see your work are accustomed to reading countless scripts in a day or week and so they are somewhat numb to the process. They know from only a few pages whether it interests them or has the requisite level of skill to be worthy of further consideration.

If you've made it over that initial hump and have successfully engaged them with your brilliant opening, it is now time to hold their interest with the scene that follows. Don't get cocky and don't let up. Work hard to maintain that connection. Your success REALLY depends on it.

If you have been doing the exercises as you are working your way through this text, you should have an opening scene, as well as the beginnings of your Road Map outline. It's time to write the scene that follows your great opening.

How you begin is easy... Ask yourself the Seven Vital Questions.
1. What needs to happen in the scene?
2. Who needs to be there and who does not?
3. Where could the scene take place?
4. How long must the scene be?
5. What might happen to surprise the audience?
6. Is the scene necessary?
7. What are some options and/or alternatives?

In addition to the Seven Vital Questions listed above, one further element to consider is the relative space you have between your opening scene and the Inciting Incident. Based on your Road Map, you should have some idea of what that is and when it will be appearing. As such, think about how this scene helps to lead you and the reader in that direction.

Got the answers? Now write!

CHAPTER 11

Editing Your Script...
Your Work Is Never Done

First Things First – Take a Break!

When you complete a draft, particularly the first draft of a screenplay, you have to walk away for at least a short time. Everyone is different... perhaps a day will be enough while others may need a few weeks, but any screenwriter who has labored through a completed script will need to unfog their brains and gain some perspective on the material as you will have been far too close to it for too long to simply jump right in without a break. I promise that if you ignore this advice, you'll overlook a lot of really poor writing in your script. Time away is necessary to

recognize the difference between your best work and the stuff that needs help. Without that, you just end up thinking every word you put down is pure genius and let's face it, we know that's not true.

THE FIRST READ

With newfound energy and a fresh mind, it's time to take a look at the material. I STRONGLY recommend reading a hard copy rather than straight off your computer screen. There are several reasons for this, but the most important is that if you are reading on your computer, it will be **100% IMPOSSIBLE** to resist making small corrections and/or changes as you go. If you see "the" missing from a sentence or ADAM spelled ADAMM you won't be able to resist. No matter how small the fix is, the constant stopping and starting will significantly break up the flow and pacing. Your goal is to make it a seamless read for others and it's critical you gauge how successful you've been in this regard. A task you can't do if you are stopping and starting as you go. Additionally, the distraction of incoming emails and so forth further adds to this problem.

When you finish the initial read, write down your general thoughts. What do you remember? What notes come to mind first? Consider some of the broader questions such as…

- Is the pacing too fast or too slow?
- If it's a comedy, ask yourself (honestly) if you laughed out loud.
- If it's an action film, was there enough excitement?
- Are the characters memorable?
- Try and identify the major plot points. Do they appear at the right time?
- Did the Climax resolve the primary conflict set up in the First Act Break?
- Does the Midpoint work as a game-changing moment in the script?
- Does it elevate the stakes, drama, and tension of the story?
- Is the Second Act Break the true low point for your protagonist?
- Is the Climax original and exciting?
- With respect to the characters, have they evolved through the script?
- Has your protagonist grown and/or changed as a result of facing whatever conflict they've had to overcome?

- Is there a great, memorable supporting character?
- Is the antagonist a true nemesis, worthy of your hero, or are they a forgettable foe in need of some further development?

Additionally, check how long it took to read the script. Depending on how fast or slow of a reader you are, you should be able to gauge whether it will be a quick or easy read for others. Did you get bogged down in certain parts? Did it drag anywhere? Were the descriptions too dense? Also, try to remember if you checked the time during the read. This may sound odd, but think about your past movie experiences. When you are really enjoying a film, do you look at your watch or even think about the time? Conversely, during a movie you're not particularly enjoying, don't you find yourself checking your watch fairly often? In many cases, an extremely long, but great film can fly by while a much shorter movie can feel like a lifetime in the theater.

When you're done, give yourself another day or two for additional clarity.

THE SECOND READ

This time, do it with a pen in hand. Make notes on the pages as you go. Mark any dialogue that feels cliché or awkward. Note scenes that don't seem effective or come off as contrived. Is there too much description? Is a scene too long or too short? Is a passage of dialogue clunky or ineffective? Does a sequence need to be more exciting or creatively delivered? Are you hating a particular character? Are his or her actions believable in a given moment?

Basically, you want to write down all the impressions that enter your mind as you read through the pages.

With experience, you will reach a point where you will naturally consider everything as you go, but in the meantime, employ a checklist encompassing the screenwriting elements you've been reading about.

A few of the big ones...

Structure	Are the act breaks where they should be?
Tone	Does it match the audience expectations?
Dialogue	Have you achieved Distinct Voice?
Characters	Do they feel authentic? Do any really pop?
The Snooze Bar	Are there any lulls to be addressed?
Coincidence	Are successes and advances earned?
Story	Do scenes appear creative or derivative?
Antagonist	Are they a worthy opponent?
Opening Scene	Does it immediately engage and elicit questions?
An Early Complication	Does it genuinely make resolving the conflict harder?
The Second Act	Is there a consistent escalation? Will it hold interest?
The Climax	Does it satisfy? Does it match the core conflict?

During both reads, you will want to pay special attention to the structure as an overly long First Act is one of the most prominent mistakes new writers make. If a page is a minute of screen time, imagine sitting in a theater and watching a movie for more than half an hour and still not knowing what it's about. I simply cannot overstate how **monumental** an error this is! Be conscious of whether you are taking too long to "hook" your audience with the core conflict of your film.

Is the Second Act too short? This is another common and related problem, particularly when you don't outline. Does the script meet whatever expectations the audience will have based on genre? Is there enough action, comedy, horror, thrills, suspense, drama, etc.? Be very aware of Distinct Voice and whether the script successfully achieves it. Do all the characters sound the same or worse, like you? Do kids sound like kids? Do people appropriately represent their personalities and do those personalities come across via the dialogue?

Are the characters dynamic and original? Do they feel authentic and not come across as stock or stereotypical? Are they memorable? Are they worthy of their name? By that, I mean could they just as easily be called COP, WAITRESS, or DOCTOR, or do they possess enough personality for your audience to care what their Momma named 'em?

The Second Act is the meat of your movie and requires the greatest amount of effort because it isn't part of the initial idea. It arrives later after much thought and development. Take note of whether your Second Act successfully creates obstacles for your protagonist along the way towards resolving the overall conflict. Do the stakes mount? Does the action increase? Are you devoting any or enough time to characters other than your protagonist? Do we see the antagonist and their motivations? Supporting characters? Are you addressing subplots sufficiently?

Another pitfall to be aware of is redundancy. This is vital because a common crutch for screenwriters who haven't successfully cracked Act 2 is to fill pages by repeating themselves. The scenes don't literally repeat, but the same lesson is learned three or four different ways; or instead of three distinct clues, the protagonist gets the same information from multiple sources. This is super annoying to readers and a waste of both their time and yours.

Take Ego Out of the Equation! This may be the most important aspect of the editing process. You don't win any prizes for having less red marks on the paper than the kid sitting next to you in class. Be your harshest critic because no one else will be prior to reaching the decision makers and if you go easy on your writing, you will be setting yourself up to fail because they won't be interested in anything less than stellar work. You have far more competition than you realize so demand excellence from yourself if you truly want even a chance at success.

TIME FOR A SECOND OPINION... PERHAPS EVEN A THIRD

First things first... make absolutely sure the opinion you solicit is one you trust. If it's a friend, significant other, or Mom, take them off the hook and tell them you want the unvarnished truth — their sincere opinion, because nothing short of that will be helpful to you beyond a quick stroking of your ego, and you won't get it otherwise. Mom won't want to hurt your feelings.

Alternatively, you may choose to hire a professional to give you an opinion. The key to this is to find someone who has actual development experience. Not simply a reader and writer of coverage, but someone who has actively participated in the development of screenplays and has worked with screenwriters. The vast majority of people offering their services and charging a great deal for coverage **DO NOT** have that experience. They have been hired in the past to read scripts and give a basic opinion as to the overall quality, but with no knowledge of how to improve them or any experience actually doing so.

They can tell you their opinion as to its commerciality, that the characters feel clichéd or the writing derivative, and perhaps that would be helpful information. However, if they can't suggest substantive ways to fix story problems, offer solutions to structural flaws, and provide insight as to how to approach the editing process, your money may very well be wasted so be careful.

WHAT IS COVERAGE?

This is a tool that has become overvalued by screenwriters, particularly less experienced ones who don't really understand what it is. Simply stated, decision makers such as executives, agents, and producers don't have time to read all the scripts that come across their desks. In order to weed out the chaff that's a waste of their time, they have assistants, mailroom staff, and even unpaid interns read scripts and write various forms of coverage.

It's essentially a book report and usually comprised of 2–4 pages. On the first page, there will be general information like title, author, date, and perhaps other elements like genre or locations. There is usually a recommend line or box that offers yes, no, or maybe. There is also a prominent logline, which is one sentence that summarizes what the script is about.

A longer, more detailed synopsis (generally 1 or 2 pages) follows, succeeded by a page of general comments. Instead of using an hour to read through a script, the decision maker can now take 5 minutes to scan the coverage and know whether to read it or have the necessary information to pass without having done so.

Now that you know what coverage is, ask yourself how it would help you and why it's worth paying for. Do you need a synopsis of your own script? You know what it's about, don't you? I understand that the comments might prove helpful, but comments in coverage have a fatal flaw: they identify problems, but they rarely offer solutions. It is one thing to suggest the characters are flimsy or the story isn't believable, but another thing entirely to suggest how to fix those issues. Furthermore, the opinion of someone who likely doesn't have extensive development experience or awareness of the difference between reading scripts and fixing them is often not worth the cost you will be paying. BUYER BEWARE.

Presentation Counts!

After the rewriting process, it is imperative you consider the appearance of your script. Is the formatting correct? Is everything where it should be? Are there unnecessary spaces or missing pages?

SPELL CHECK! Let me repeat that: SPELL CHECK!
I'm sorry, one more time... **SPEL CHEQUE!**

Considering how easy it is these days to have correct spelling, it's really annoying when it is overlooked. It may all seem trivial, but anything that stops a reader and breaks up the flow is bad for you — and these are flaws that are pretty easy to avoid.

KEYS TO REMEMBER

- You might notice that a recurring trend in these notes is screenwriters tend to be in a hurry to finish which results in mistakes that more time and patience would remedy. One such case is that when screenwriters complete a first draft, they are often so convinced it's fantastic they don't even bother to edit. No need to explain the error of that decision, but those who do edit, tend to dive into that process right away in an effort to reach a finish line that appears to be so close they can touch it.
- No writer of any level of experience, upon completing a script that takes days, weeks, or many months to complete, has the objective frame of mind to properly evaluate the work immediately. TAKE A BREAK!
- The first read should never be on your computer screen. You need to absorb the script like a reader would and avoid stopping and starting as you go.
- You will be far better served by marking ALL the places that need work, mistakes that require fixing, and issues that must be considered and addressed, rather than attending to them one at a time as you go.
- It cannot be stressed enough that structural mistakes, especially an overly long First Act, MUST be addressed. It will be hard enough to get industry professionals to read past page 10 of less-than-stellar work, but you simply cannot expect them to stick with a script that more than 30 pages in has yet to establish a core conflict and a discernable plot.
- You cannot be arrogant or overly sensitive during this phase of the process. Stay open to change and consider all the alternatives. Take other opinions to heart. You don't have to agree with them, but recognize that fresh eyes often see more clearly.
- **Be your harshest critic!**

WRITING EXERCISE:
CAN YOU REALLY DO A BETTER JOB?

How many times have you walked out of theater annoyed or turned off your television in frustration after seeing a movie that disappointed you? Have you ever thought to yourself that you could have done a better job? You're reading this because you have an interest in movies and specifically screenwriting, so I'm betting the answer is yes.

There are a number of reasons why a film turns out poorly and rarely is it as simple as the script wasn't what it needed to be, but for the purposes of this exercise, let's assume that's the case.

Choose three films you thought had decent to great ideas, but you were disappointed with the execution. Not bad acting or directing, but ones where you felt the story and/or plotting weren't right or were flawed.

You have two options now. You can simply re-watch the films or, if you're feeling particularly bold and willing to put forth some effort, go online or to a public library and get your hands on one or more of the screenplays. You'll be surprised at how many are readily available with a simple Internet search.

Don't worry about proper formatting as the script you get your hands on may have been altered for publishing or some other reason. Focus on the content and break it down. Ask all the relevant questions about structure, character, dialogue, etc. What are the best and worst aspects of the script? What would you change? How? See if you can identify the script's greatest failing or the element that most ruined the movie for you. Is it a character you particularly didn't respond to, or perhaps you found the Second Act boring. Maybe things came too easily to the protagonist and he or she didn't earn their triumphs.

If you really want to practice, go ahead and outline how you would improve it. I won't advocate actually rewriting anything because you don't own the characters or material, but if it is simply for practice and executed with that understanding in mind, it certainly won't hurt you to do so.

Presentation Matters…
The Gatekeepers

I t's time to delve a bit deeper into why proper formatting and the appearance of your script is so important.

Above and beyond the obvious, the simple truth is that your script will very likely have to pass through at least one, if not multiple gatekeepers before it is read by an actual decision maker. Executives, agents, and producers that you are hoping will read your work and transform your life simply don't have the time to wade through all of the scripts that you and everyone like you are submitting. Optimistically maybe 10% of their day is allocated to new material, and most of that will be scripts coming from established writers and submitted by their well-known representatives.

If they are agents or managers, they are servicing their client's scripts or finding their clients new jobs. If they are executives or producers, they are focused on films already in development or production. It may be jarring to hear this, but accept that your script doesn't matter to any of these people in the slightest.

For every 100 unrepresented and unsolicited scripts that land on their desks, the odds are maybe 1 and perhaps even ZERO are good enough to be a movie. Long odds! I know — your script is the exception. Newsflash — everyone thinks they are the one, just like everyone who shows up to audition for *American Idol* thinks they have the talent to be a rock star and we've all seen those episodes.

The decision makers can't waste their time reading 99 scripts they'll be passing on to find 1 they may like. Hence the need for gatekeepers who come in many shapes and sizes. Junior executives, assistants, mailroom staff, freelance readers, and often interns fill this role. They read the scripts, perhaps write some form of coverage, and in most cases, provide their boss all the necessary information to pass while sounding like they've read it themselves.

You can imagine how tedious it is to read one bad script after another. Gatekeepers quickly acquire an eye for the signs of a bad script without having read a single page. When a hard copy comes in with art and illustrations or incorrect binding or a hard or digital copy has odd fonts and colors, the first thought is this person didn't take the time to learn what a script should look like so what are the chances they took the time to learn how to write one properly? Even if yours is the exception and the script is fantastic, you've already predisposed the reader against you. Not a good start.

The next thing a gatekeeper will check before reading is the page count. Don't kid yourselves into thinking otherwise. **ALL** gatekeepers check the page count. They dread reading bad scripts, but they hate LONG, bad scripts even more. Now not all long scripts are bad scripts, but if a gatekeeper sees that a script is 125 or more pages, you have once again biased them against you. Odds are (and they definitely play the odds) that you've written a snooze fest.

Many factors will inform your eventual page count and if it's appropriate that you submit 120 pages, then so be it, but as an aspiring screenwriter, you're more likely to sell *Wedding Crashers*, *Scream*, or *The Fast and the Furious* at 90–110 than *Gandhi*, *Kramer vs. Kramer*, or *Schindler's List* at 120+. This is another consideration to factor in when selecting that first concept. No one says you can't write a long, sweeping drama or the next great historical epic, but it probably shouldn't be your first effort. When you're trying to break down the door, give yourself the best chance to get it open.

Most submissions are done digitally now, which makes formatting of greater importance, but if you are sending a hard copy of a spec, it should be on three hole punched, white paper, held in place by TWO 1.25-inch brass fasteners, also known as brads, in the top and bottom holes. **Leave the middle hole empty.** This simple binding allows for easy reading and more importantly, easy photocopying, which is a VERY good thing for you. Copying means more people are going to be reading your script and trust me, you want that.

DO NOT send your script in a three ring binder. DO NOT stick loose script pages into a folder. DO NOT use a giant black clip on the top or side. In many years of being a gatekeeper and then using gatekeepers, I have seen each of these countless times and I NEVER once recommended or saw a script submitted like this recommended for further consideration.

If you are inclined to include pictures, photographs, and/or illustrations with a screenplay, regardless of how it is submitted, make certain that there is true purpose and an undeniable benefit to doing so. Your script needs to be able to stand on its own without accessorizing. Don't cut a few random pictures out of magazines and think that will make a difference. Storyboards can be cool and other sorts of quality imagery can spark some interest, in part because they demonstrate genuine effort, but with few exceptions, my advice would be to let your writing be the featured work.

Finally, your script should be in 12-point Courier or Courier Final Draft. It is the modern equivalent of the original typewriter font and more importantly, the font that every professional screenwriter uses. There are no points for originality if you stray from this.

The gatekeepers haven't even read page 1 yet and you can see how many potential mistakes could have been made to already limit, if not completely destroy your chances of getting past the velvet rope.

One of the reasons these mistakes are so common is that many aspiring or novice screenwriters model their first efforts off scripts they have managed to get their hands on. They don't realize that many scripts found online or seen in books, magazines, and other sources, are reformatted to fit a different layout or altered to minimize page counts and other elements. Additionally, many, if not most of these available drafts are production drafts that include scene numbering, camera angles and shots, music selections, and other elements that should NOT be included in a spec script.

A shooting script is great for reading, but it is notably different from a spec. When you emulate production drafts and include shot selections, specific songs, and scene numbering, you are doing other people's jobs for them. Moreover, you don't know how to properly do those jobs so it is doubly wrong. You need to understand that it isn't your role to determine what's in closeup or to call for a medium or crane shot. The director is tasked with shooting the movie and is therefore responsible for deciding what shots to use and when.

YOUR MOVIE'S TITLE

The importance of a great title should go without saying. *The Shawshank Redemption* is a spectacular film, but we can all agree the title is awful. This is a film that is rated by many amongst the top 100 movies of all time. It was nominated for multiple Oscars including Best Picture and despite all this, was a disappointment at the box office due in many experts' opinion to consumer confusion associated with the title. How many people might have gone to the theater to see it if they had some idea of what it was about?

The Coen Brothers are tremendously gifted filmmakers whose immense contributions to cinema cannot be argued, but their titles are a mixed bag, some great and others not so much. *The Hudsucker Proxy*, *Barton Fink*, and even cult favorite *The Big Lebowski* rate as head-scratchers for many people and likely made marketing the films much more challenging. This certainly isn't an indictment of the quality of these movies, quite the contrary, but there's little question that *Fargo, O Brother, Where Art Thou?*, and *Raising Arizona* generated far more interest from moviegoers off the titles alone.

Why is this important for you? Much as a movie's title can substantially help to draw audiences to the theater, a script's title has the same power to either generate interest or conversely, to confuse a potential reader.

> *"You never get a second chance to make a first impression."*
>
> — Will Rogers

So what makes a great title? First and foremost — simplicity. You don't want a mouthful. It should be evocative and suggestive of your concept or your tone. Consider the mileage you get from *The 40-Year-Old Virgin* or *Fatal Attraction*. How about *Kill Bill* or *The Hangover?* Simple, clear, and most importantly, they all drive the individual to want answers. They make you want to sit in a theater. That's your goal and must be the question you ask yourself when testing possible titles. Does this make me want to go to the movies?

You should tend to avoid proper names unless it's a name people are familiar with such as JFK or Robin Hood. *Jerry Maguire* only works when you see a poster with Tom Cruise on it; otherwise who would care? Consider movies like *Donnie Brasco, Michael Collins*, or *Mary Reilly*. All are films with A list talent, but none make you want to get off the couch and head to the cinema.

THE TITLE PAGE

Don't get creative with fonts and colors. Use the same font as the rest of the script: 12 point Courier. Your title should be centered, approximately one third of the way down the page. Do not add marketing slogans or taglines. Once again, not your job and chances are, it won't help your cause, but it can hurt it.

Centered below your title will be Screenplay by and your name. If there are two writers, working as a team, place Screenplay by on one line and centered below it, place the names John Smith & Bob Jones. Use an ampersand (&), not AND as they mean different things. An ampersand in screenwriting denotes a writing team while the word AND means two writers worked on the script separately, one rewriting the other, but both still receiving credit.

If you register your script with the Writers Guild (recommended — do so online at wga.org) then it is at your discretion to write WGA Registered (Writers Guild of America) on the bottom left of the page. It neither helps nor hurts.

Place your contact information such as your phone number and/or email on the bottom right of the page. Make it easy for them to reach you with good news!

DO NOT indicate what draft it is such as First Draft or Third Draft or Second Draft Revised. Not only does no one care, but any spec script, regardless of whether it is your fourth draft or your eighty-third, will be considered a First Draft by anyone who buys it. Moreover, people will wonder why you are submitting a first draft or conversely, needed three or four to get it right. You can't win. DO NOT date your script or title page for much the same reason. Nobody wants yesterday's material. It cannot help you and it will absolutely hurt you the older that date gets. It isn't important or relevant information for a reader to have. If you sell a script, future drafts will be dated as part of the development and production process, but that's okay... there's a logical reason for this AND you've already been paid!

It would be foolish to suggest even for a moment that the content of your script isn't the most important thing, but ignoring these simple things is the best, fastest, and dumbest way to make sure the content you've worked so hard on fails to be properly evaluated.

An example of a proper title page ...

Money in the Bank

Screenplay by
John Smith & Bob Jones

WGA Registered   John Smith
                                              (310)555-1234
                                              smithy@yes.com

No Speed Bumps

Just as it is important that your title page and the general appearance of your script LOOK professional, I can't emphasize enough how important it is that your writing READ as professional. You're gunning for the major leagues and with a spec, perhaps your top priority, aside

from the execution, is to submit work that reads seamlessly. No speed bumps! The more a gatekeeper or decision maker needs to stop and start while looking at your work, the more likely they won't continue past the first few pages. Despite  what Delroy Lindo says in *Get Shorty* or what you may have seen in other scripts, misspelled words, incorrect punctuation, and the ignorance of the rules of grammar won't win you any fans or prizes.

Not knowing the difference between *you're* and *your* or *its* and *it's* is simply not acceptable, especially for anyone with a modicum of intelligence who wishes to be a professional writer and has access to spell check, Wikipedia, dictionary, and thesaurus.com, and the myriad of other resources freely available. If grammar and spelling aren't your forte, get a friend or two or ten to proofread your work before it gets sent out. If you want to be taken seriously, your work absolutely MUST warrant that.

NO EXCUSES... because anything less and **you're** wasting **your** time.

Hopefully, you are using professional screenwriting software, which will do most of the formatting work for you. If you don't care to spend the money on Final Draft, free software is readily available online. I can't begin to say how much easier it is to write with screenwriting software versus Word or some other word processing application. If not, you will spend a ridiculous and entirely unnecessary amount of time using your TAB button and setting margins.

The font should be 12-point Courier. Do not use other fonts for added emphasis. This is the industry standard. Use it. If you choose to **bold**, <u>underline</u>, or *italicize* anything, do so sparingly. To do so occasionally can provide necessary, desired, and useful emphasis on a particular word or phrase while overuse removes the effect and becomes an annoying distraction.

Page numbering is important in screenplays and should always be included. They should be placed in the upper right corner with a period. Do not number the first page.

DO NOT use scene numbers. As stated previously, this is only something that should be included in production drafts and shooting scripts. They do not belong in spec screenplays.

SO IT BEGINS...

FADE IN: This is how your script should start. It is the traditional opening of any feature screenplay. It is left-justified as though it were a scene heading.

In the case that you open with narration over a black screen, your script would begin with BLACKNESS, left-justified and in all caps. Then NARRATOR as a character slug with dialogue done normally. There would be a (V.O.) next to the character slug, which stands for voiceover and will be discussed later. Prior to the first image on screen, you would then insert the FADE IN:.

"FROM THE DAWN OF TIME WE CAME, MOVING SILENTLY DOWN THROUGH THE CENTURIES. LIVING MANY SECRET LIVES, STRUGGLING TO REACH THE TIME OF THE GATHERING WHEN THE FEW WHO REMAIN WILL BATTLE TO THE LAST. NO ONE HAS EVER KNOWN WE WERE AMONG YOU... UNTIL NOW."

– *SEAN CONNERY, HIGHLANDER*

```
BLACKNESS

                         NARRATOR (V.O.)
                Once upon a time, there lived a
                beautiful princess...

FADE IN:

INT. CASTLE - DAY

The great hall echoes with the footsteps of a horde of
visitors, anxious for the King's arrival. They all
commiserate and plot, seeking opportunity and fortune.

A TRUMPET sounds!

                         HERALD
                All hail the King!
```

You might also choose to begin with a title card over a black screen. In that case, you would also begin with BLACKNESS, left-justified and in all caps, followed by TITLE CARD:, left-justified like a scene heading. Then write the content of the card in ALL CAPS as though it were dialogue with no character slug. Prior to the first image appearing on screen, you would then insert the FADE IN:.

```
BLACKNESS

TITLE CARD: AN UNCHARTED ISLAND TWO YEARS FROM TOMORROW

FADE IN:

EXT. BEACH - SUNSET
```

If in either of the above cases, the narration and/or title card appear over imagery rather than a black screen, the FADE IN: would come first, followed by a scene heading and description of what was visible on screen. Then the narration or title card would be inserted.

```
FADE IN:

EXT. MARTIAN LANDSCAPE - DAY

The red clay sand on the planet's surface vibrates as
something massive approaches.

TITLE CARD:    MARS   2025 AD

                         NARRATOR (V.O.)
                Five years have passed since the
                solar flares sent humanity
                underground. The last, best hope
                for mankind would soon be within
                reach, but the forces of Lord
                Kermit and his evil muppet minions
                are determined to intervene.
```

CREDIT SEQUENCES

You will see many, many scripts that identify where and when to place opening credit sequences. **DO NOT** do this!

It is not your decision to make. Novice screenwriters often get creative, particularly with opening credit sequences, crafting some sort of Bond movie opening, followed by very specific placement of credits. There may not even be opening credits in your film. Many no longer have them, saving everything for the end, including the major stars and director. This is a directorial choice and not something to concern yourself with, especially at this stage of the process. Trust me when I say that no one cares where you want the credits placed. Also, next time you are reading the credits of a film, note where it says Title Design by and think about that person whose job you are trying to steal away.

KEYS TO REMEMBER

- There is very little margin for error in screenwriting, particularly with first or early efforts designed to gain you entry into the professional ranks.
- This is especially true when you consider how many other writers and screenplays are competing for attention. Poor execution is an obvious flaw, but poor presentation can be just as much of a killer and is easily avoided with minimal effort.
- If you want to be treated like a professional, you better look the part!
- Don't model your script and especially its format off of non-spec screenplays such as production drafts that are often available online as they include numerous elements that should not be in your work. Doing so is an early indicator that you don't know what you are doing, and sending such signals as early as page 1 is never a recipe for success.
- The title is your first chance to market your work. Don't waste the opportunity.
- Professional writers make mistakes like anyone else, but their scripts are never littered with grammatical and spelling errors that are easy to fix and avoid. One of the surest ways to not only look like an amateur, but a poor writer with little talent, is to submit a script that appears to have been written by a 5th grader.
- Presentation may not be as important as your content, but in the professional environment of Hollywood, any failure in this area often has the power to guarantee your content never even gets read. You simply cannot afford to be myopic, stubborn, or lazy about this issue.

WRITING EXERCISE: Back to School

This chapter is largely about professionalism and the idea that if you want to be taken seriously as a screenwriter, you need to do whatever it takes to prevent easily avoidable errors and mistakes that prove you are anything but.

Amateur work simply will not suffice.

Anyone can learn how to hit a baseball, but that doesn't mean they can play in the pros, and it certainly doesn't mean they can jack a 90 mph curve ball over the green monster in Fenway. It's very important that you recognize this analogy isn't an exaggeration. The number of people who can write a great script may be significantly larger than the number who can hit a home run, but both require more than just a passing interest and neither can be achieved easily or quickly.

That means this will require a lot of hard work. Good writers, especially professional ones, do research. They don't just guess or presume to know all the facts. You have to become an expert on the places, people, and subjects you explore in your work. So let's do some research!

Refer back to the writing exercise from the Concept chapter.

Pick one of your "What If?" scenarios, one of the odd or obscure jobs, and one of the locations. I won't tell you to become the world's leading authority, but go beyond the Wikipedia pages. Learn about the city, its population, people, customs, landmarks, etc.… Where might you place some scenes?

Maybe try and connect with someone who has the job and get some genuine insight. The "What If?" scenario may not be an actual event like JFK's assassination, but there will still be topics to investigate. If there's buried treasure, where might it have come from? Instead of a treasure chest of assorted jewels, is there an explanation for how a lost Mark Twain manuscript could be there? Get creative.

If you want to learn about something else, by all means, choose that instead. Pretend you're back in school and writing a term paper, only have some fun with a topic that truly interests you and smile because you won't need footnotes or a bibliography to get an A!

CHAPTER 13

The Elements of a Scene...
Amateur vs. Professional

There are five elements to any scene in a spec screenplay.
1. SCENE HEADINGS aka SCENE SLUGS
2. DESCRIPTION aka ACTION
3. CHARACTER SLUGS
4. DIALOGUE
5. TRANSITIONS

AN IMPORTANT NOTE before delving into the elements of a scene and one that will be referenced repeatedly throughout this section. One of your primary goals should be to limit your script to only those words that are absolutely necessary to deliver the best possible experience and make an excellent impression.

It would honestly shock you to see the difference an experienced screenwriter can make by just editing out the excess noise from a script that many would deem ready for submission. I've seen 20 pages get cut without altering anything in the plot. It's the exact same script, just thinner. This tightening of the belt so to speak will dramatically increase and improve the pacing of your script, as well as the ease of the read. Imagine how much healthier you'd feel at your optimum weight.

How much more endurance you'd have. How much more energy you'd exude. It's the same with your writing.

I will suggest several times cutting as little as a single word or line and while individually, these cuts wouldn't make much of a difference, I PROMISE you that over the course of a full feature screenplay, they add up to multiple pages. Cutting them leads to a different, far more engaging final product.

Scene Headings aka Scene Slugs

There will always be something on screen; as the screenwriter, you must indicate at all times where and when the image is taking place. Scene Headings begin with either INT. or EXT., representing either interior or exterior — inside or outside.

Any enclosed space from a bedroom to an airplane to a cave would be an interior location. Exterior locations include anything outside such as an open road, the Atlantic Ocean, or the surface of the moon. Sometimes, it can be tricky. If a character is sitting on the deck of a yacht, that would be an EXT. If they travel below deck to a stateroom, that is an INT. If they are driving in a convertible mustang, it depends on whether the scene is EXT. ROAD and we are watching the car move or INT. MUSTANG CONVERTIBLE and we are with the character as they sing along with the radio.

In the case of a car, plane, or other vehicle, it is either INT. PLANE or EXT. SKY. If the image on screen is of the vehicle, then it is an EXT., followed by SKY, HIGHWAY, PACIFIC OCEAN, or whatever the location. In the case that the action is actually on the outside of a vehicle such as a fight on the roof of a train, then it would be EXT. TRAIN ROOF.

The one anomaly is when the action is underwater. You can decide for yourself if that is an interior or exterior, but in those instances, simply slug UNDERWATER without an INT. or EXT. The reader will understand. Some examples:

```
INT. CONVERTIBLE MUSTANG
INT. PAWN SHOP
INT. RICO'S HABERDASHERY
INT. SPACE STATION
EXT. ROAD
EXT. TRAIN ROOF
EXT. SKY
EXT. SHADY ACRES NURSING HOME
EXT. GOLDEN GATE BRIDGE
BLACK SCREEN
UNDERWATER
```

Some say the scene heading for the Eiffel Tower should look like this:

```
EXT. PARIS — EIFFEL TOWER
```

I disagree. If the reader doesn't already know the action is in Paris, either state it in the description or assume that they are smart enough to know where the Eiffel Tower, the Empire State Building, or the Great Pyramids are. Some things should go without saying.

Similarly, if you are in one part of a larger location such as the dugout of Fenway Park or the master bedroom of Joe's House, some would suggest this:

```
EXT. FENWAY PARK — DUGOUT
INT. JOE'S HOUSE — MASTER BEDROOM
```

Again, I would not. In the case of the dugout, set the scene as FENWAY PARK and then use the description to detail that the action is focused in the dugout. Alternatively, if the reader already knows the action is in Fenway Park from a previous scene such as arriving at the stadium, slug it as the DUGOUT because FENWAY PARK thus becomes redundant. This is the likelier scenario. In the case of a house, the same rules apply. If we already know it's Joe's house, simply slug it as MASTER BEDROOM or even better JOE'S BEDROOM, either of which are far simpler for the reader.

If you do use multiple locations in one slug, separate them with a space, a hyphen, and another space. Do NOT do any of the following:

```
EXT. THE GREAT PYRAMID/EGYPT
INT. VIP BOX AT MADISON SQUARE GARDEN
INT. THE MASTER BEDROOM IN JOE'S HOUSE
```

There will be instances where clarity is helpful and worth having such as in the following examples with proper format:

```
EXT. WAL-MART — LOADING DOCK
EXT. JOE'S HOUSE — BACK YARD
INT. AIRPLANE — FIRST CLASS
```

Do not say inside or outside after INT. or EXT. It is redundant.

```
INT. INSIDE THE EMPIRE STATE BUILDING
EXT. OUTSIDE JOE'S HOUSE
```

When you are moving through multiple rooms in a larger location such as the rooms of a house or the streets of Manhattan, it is not necessary to individually slug each location as you go. The reader will understand you are going from the kitchen to the dining room via the description or that you are traveling through Times Square to Broadway. To slug each of these would become a major distraction. Don't interrupt important content to slug a new location the reader is already aware of based on the description. Consider the car chase through San Francisco in *The Rock*. Can you imagine how slowly and poorly it would read if every street during that chase were individually slugged? It would take ten times longer to read the scene than watch it. NEVER a good thing.

The final element of a scene heading is the time of day. Don't use an actual time such as 3:43 AM or 12 o'clock. The purpose isn't to literally indicate an exact time, but rather, to provide a deeper sense of the location such as DAY or NIGHT. A viewer wouldn't know it was 3:43 AM without a clock. Other options include MORNING, EVENING, AFTERNOON, DUSK, or some other **simple** moniker, but I would never use more than one word. Quite often, you'll go from one scene to the next in real time. In those cases, you can also use CONTINUOUS instead of a time of day to make that fact clearer. For example, if you traveled from the front yard into a house, CONTINUOUS would be used. If the action moved from a hotel room to the elevator to the lobby, those too would use CONTINUOUS.

There will be cases where the time of day won't be relevant such as inside a cave or submarine. In those instances, it is your choice to include the time of day if you choose, or simply leave it blank.

```
INT. MORTY'S HOUSE OF PAIN — DAY
INT. THE CHEESECAKE FACTORY — EVENING
INT. PRISON CELL — MORNING
INT. CAVE
EXT. MONASTERY — CONTINUOUS
EXT. GARDEN OF EDEN — SUNSET
EXT. THE RIVER STYX — NIGHT
EXT. LAGOON — SUNRISE
```

Other sources suggest certain elements for a scene heading such as indicating if a vehicle is moving or stationary, or including a season such as winter or a year like 2064 in parentheses after the location or time of day. I vehemently disagree with all of this. Scene slugs have one function and that is to indicate visually the location and setting of a scene. Summer or 1962 are nonspecific and should be placed with other details in the description, as that's what it's for. Even then, only if that information is relevant to the scene. Don't ask a gatekeeper to read or remember more than what's necessary.

There will be occasions when you go back and forth between an INT. and EXT. such as someone inside a car stopping to ask someone on the street for directions or a mother inside a house talking to her husband who is raking leaves in the front yard. In cases such as this, slug each scene once, then do the dialogue as if it were one scene. Don't distract the reader with lots of unnecessary scene headings going back and forth.

Here is an example:

```
INT. MUSTANG - DAY

George sees a WOMAN, walking her dog and stops next
to her.


EXT. ROAD - CONTINUOUS

The woman turns to George as he LOWERS his window.

                    GEORGE
          Excuse me, do you know where
          the nearest IHOP is?

                    WOMAN
          Geez, sorry. Can't help you.

                    GEORGE
          Sorry to hear that. I'm
          jonesing for a stack of jacks!

The dog BARKS.

                    GEORGE
          Looks like he agrees.

                    WOMAN
          Actually, she's more of a
          waffles kinda gal.

                    GEORGE
          Sorry to hear that.

                    WOMAN
          If you're not partial, there's
          a Denny's two miles West.

                    GEORGE
          Oh no, only the hop for me.

                    WOMAN
          Okay then. Well, good luck with
          that.

The woman yanks her dog and hurries away from George.
```

NOTE how much easier the scene reads without the addition of scene headings between each piece of dialogue. It also makes it a 1 page scene instead of 2.

A final note on scene headings is that they should NEVER be the last line on a page. Screenwriting software **should** take care of this for you, but if you aren't using it or it fails to do so, and there isn't room for proper spacing and at least one line of description under the scene heading, simply place it at the top of the subsequent page.

DESCRIPTION AKA ACTION

The second element of a scene and the one where LESS IS MORE is most relevant. First, you must realize that the majority of readers, and especially gatekeepers, will either skim or skip your description. They've seen it all before and much of it isn't necessary to understand what's going on. It helps create an atmosphere and hopefully enhances a script, but it can also serve to ruin one when it's long, overly descriptive, and unnecessarily dense, an issue that plagues far too many early screenwriting efforts. You're writing a screenplay, not a novel. Don't forget it!

Do you want to be an interior decorator or write a movie? It's a question that comes up A LOT with screenwriters. How important do you think it is when you slug a scene in a bedroom to include the color scheme, the type of furniture, the square footage, or the artist who painted the picture hanging over the bed?

This is from an actual script and an example of what NOT to do:

```
INT. LISA'S BEDROOM - NIGHT

The 15 X 20 foot bedroom is tastefully decorated with
matching, maple furniture resting on a pale, red
carpet. Plush linens and pillows perfectly match the
décor. Under the high ceiling, three large windows
flank the bed on the right, each allowing just the
perfect amount of moonlight to pierce through the
ecru, Venetian blinds that have been three quarters
closed. A large Sony plasma screen television hangs
opposite the bed and adjacent a dramatic, abstract
Kandinsky original and reflects Lisa as she returns
from the bathroom and climbs under her Egyptian cotton
sheets.
```

This is the extreme, as in extremely terrible, but it makes the point quite well. If you write like this, your script will be long, boring, and in a pile to be passed on before you can say verbose three times fast.

Instead, try it like this:

```
INT. LISA'S BEDROOM - NIGHT

Pottery Barn perfect.

Moonlight shines on Lisa as she climbs into bed.
```

The difference should be pretty clear. You've saved time and space, but more importantly, what have you lost? Sony product placement?

This kind of excessive detail is both common and especially useless when it comes to locations that readers, like everyone else, are substantially familiar with. Examples include hospital rooms, classrooms, bedrooms, hotel rooms, courtrooms, police stations, churches, and the DMV to name a few. Obviously, a church can be large and elegant, or small and filthy. As such, some detail may be required, mostly focusing on what sets it apart, but we've all seen cop shows and been to a doctor's office. What about the DMV? Couldn't you just say... ?

```
INT. DMV - DAY

Bureaucratic hell. Long lines and impatient faces.
```

What more is necessary? It shouldn't take more than 1–3 lines and I mean lines, not sentences, to set a mood and convey an image. Don't bog down a reader in long descriptive text that serves your ego more than the script. This is screenwriting. You're not gunning for Oprah's book club.

Redundancy is another common mistake to be on the lookout for.

```
INT. HOSPITAL - AFTERNOON

Bobby enters the hospital.
```

No kidding! Where else would he be entering?

```
INT. HOSPITAL - AFTERNOON

Bobby enters.
```

Far worse examples like this one from an actual script are quite common as well.

```
EXT. DIVE PLATFORM - MORNING

Max and Jane are standing on the dive platform,
readying their dive gear. Max puts on his dive gear,
then helps Jane on with her dive gear. Now ready to go,
Max and Jane jump off the dive platform into the sea.
```

This is annoying to read and you wouldn't believe how common it is.

Don't be that writer! How about this instead:

```
EXT. DIVE PLATFORM - MORNING

Max and Jane help each other on with their gear, then
splash into the water.
```

Make the read as **seamless** as possible. One method is to avoid long sentences with lots of "ands," "yets," and "buts" thrown in, as well as excessive punctuation. The writing should be vivid, but not necessarily poetic.

```
Sonya enters her house and navigates her way from the
foyer into the living room. When she arrives, the
shock on her face is clear and her jaw hits the floor
when she sees a full grown, gigantic moose along with
two equally huge reindeer. Inexplicably, the animals
are watching The Price is Right on her television.
```

Instead, try something like this:

```
Sonya enters and her jaw hits the floor as she spies
an enormous moose and two reindeer watching television.
```

Or for added emphasis, but only if the scene warrants the extra lines:

```
Sonya enters. What the hell!?

An enormous moose and two reindeer…

They're watching The Price is Right!
```

See how much easier these last two examples are to read than the first one. That's the key. As much as you can, make the read fast, easy, and fun.

Simplify your description wherever possible. One way to do this is to replace passive statements like `John is sitting` or `Kevin begins to exit` with more active lines like `John sits` or `Kevin exits`.

Along the same lines, replace common verbs with more descriptive, evocative choices. Instead of `Vivian walks across the foyer`, try alternatives like `saunters`, `sashays`, `glides`, `stumbles`, or trips. In the dive platform example, I replaced Max and Jane jumping into the water with `splash in`. It's just a bit more engaging.

Avoid using **adverbs**, often seen as a writer's crutch, in favor of more aggressive verbs. Instead of saying `Mark moves quickly across the battlefield`, try `Mark blasts across the battlefield` or `Mark thunders across the battlefield`.

For added emphasis, use ALL CAPS. Any kind of **significant** sound or noise should be capitalized, as should key action verbs or even phrases. Doing so allows readers who are skimming to key on certain words and phrases that warrant special emphasis and still understand the action without reading every word.

```
Tyler KNOCKS on the stage door.
Denise RINGS the bell.
Willy SPLASHES back into the water.
Brandon WHISTLES to his buddy.
```

Imagine you're a reader and you are skimming through the description. If you saw only the 3 words in ALL CAPS below, would you know what was going on?

```
The plane PLUNGES toward the ground, its
engines WHINING as FLAMES engulf the fuselage.
```

Do you have any doubt that by simply reading the words PLUNGES, WHINING, and FLAMES that you wouldn't know that a plane was on fire and going down? How about if you already knew the scene was on a plane, which you likely would, depending on the context?

You should NOT capitalize common items like a bottle of wine, a car, or a credit card if they are interchangeable and the brand or type is of no consequence.

HOWEVER, if it is important that the card be AMERICAN EXPRESS or the car specifically be a `1967 PONTIAC GTO`... ALL CAPS!

```
The carjacker fires a GLOCK 9MM at the cops.
His date looks amazing in her VALENTINO gown.
```

Bailey fires up his APPLE POWERBOOK.
Ebenezer sits in a chair, quietly reading DAVID
COPPERFIELD.

A CHARACTER'S FIRST APPEARANCE

The first time ANY character is introduced in the description, their name should appear in ALL CAPS. You should also note that every time you name a character, particularly when you provide both a first and last name, you are essentially telling the reader they are important and need to be remembered.

Look to minimize confusion and assist your reader by making sure characters that aren't important are treated as such. Call them MAN, COP, THUG, DOCTOR, LIBRARIAN, STONER DUDE, etc.

INT. BAR - NIGHT

PSYCHO FRAT BOY slams a WAITER over the head with a
bottle. Kevin and RICO, 23, race for the exit.

So in this example above, Rico is being introduced for the first time while Kevin is not. We are also seeing psycho frat boy and waiter for the first time, but we know that neither is really important beyond the function they are serving in that particular scene.

When introducing a character of significance, you should also give an indication of their age, any specific characteristics that are necessary, and perhaps something to provide insight into their personality.

As to age, you might put 40s, 40ish, or early forties instead of an actual number if you don't wish to be as specific. Some people place the age inside ( ) which is also acceptable. The one caveat is that whatever method you choose, be consistent. Don't switch back and forth.

SEBASTIAN (43)...
SEBASTIAN, early forties...
SEBASTIAN, 40s...

```
INT. DEN - EVENING

SEBASTIAN, 43, enters. His blue mohawk snags on the
beaded curtain as he steps forward, sending thousands
of tiny balls ECHOING off the wood floor.

All eyes fix on him. He shifts awkwardly under their
collective gaze.
```

While this description doesn't specify height or weight, the reader would know his age and have a sense of his physical appearance because the mohawk suggests he's not likely wearing a suit and tie. Since he shifts awkwardly rather than ignores it or laughs, there is a sense that he might lack confidence or be a little insecure.

Use common sense AND some creativity when it comes to naming your characters. If you name three guys Tom, Dick, and Harry, odds aren't great the reader will remember who's who. Alternatively, if they are Dennis, Big Mo, and Roscoe, your chances improve significantly. Be thoughtful and don't settle for the easily forgettable. Imagine if Indiana Jones was actually Bob Wilson.

Another note with regards to character names is if you introduce the character Dylan Waters, don't sometimes refer to him as Dylan and other times as Waters. Consistency staves off confusion and aids the reader.

SHOW ME, DON'T TELL ME

This concept is an enormously vital topic with regards to description. While you are writing a script, most people will watch it, not read it (we hope). You simply cannot make statements in the description that can't be visualized.

You cannot say Raymond is haunted by the memories of his accident. How do I see that? What does that look like on a movie screen?

You can get away with statements like `Reed is livid` or `Cooper is ecstatic` because an actor can play those emotions. Nevertheless, it would be significantly better if you provide a gesture or action — something visual that further highlights that emotion for the audience.

As an example, say `Reed's face flushes bright red and his body shakes in anger` or `Cooper's smile lights up as he hears the news.` These are visual and show emotion, rather than telling it.

What do these look like?

`Jack is hopelessly in love with Diane.`

`The Devil is furious at losing Walter's soul.`

`Joe lies in bed, imagining how he will spend his millions.`

`The treacherous hike will get easier on the other side of the mountain.`

`Billy can't wait to wake up tomorrow.`

`Ginger loathes the rain.`

`Regis is jealous of Cindy's new car.`

Would any of these statements be filmed? So why are they in the script? You MUST write visually.

The use, or more precisely, the overuse of **pronouns** is also something to watch and avoid. One of your goals is to craft a read that is smooth, effortless, and fun. As such, confusion in any form is your enemy. Lots of he, she, they, we, etc., will make it extremely difficult for the reader to follow. Worse, you don't want them to have to turn back pages to understand who is doing what on screen.

Don't say He enters or She crosses the street. Say Curtis enters or Denise crosses the street.

At the same time, you must also be very careful not to overuse proper names in dialogue. This too, is quite common, but fixing the first problem only to then suffer the second is basically a wash. It's a fine line between the two and you will need to learn to navigate it, but the goal is to eliminate confusion with the overuse of pronouns in description and make the dialogue sound natural by avoiding the overuse of proper names.

As an example, people don't usually call out a person's name repeatedly throughout a conversation. It may look okay, but it won't sound right.

Read this example OUT LOUD, which may seem extreme, but I promise you is not. This type of thing is done unconsciously and then overlooked by writers when they go back to edit.

```
                STACY
        Boomer, what time is it?

                BOOMER
        It's 7:30.

                STACY
        Great, well Boomer we should go
        if we don't want to be late.

                BOOMER
        We've got plenty of time.
        Don't worry.

                STACY
        No, Boomer. Listen to me, it's
        time to leave!
```

Awkward, right? Does that sound like natural conversation? This type of overuse of a name is far more common than you think.

The following is a very small issue and rare, but again, the goal is to avoid speed bumps so don't end a line with an abbreviated word and a period. It will appear to the reader as the end of a sentence and cause a minor bump in the road as seen in the top version. The second one shows the simple fix which is to simply move the abbreviated word to the beginning of the next line.

```
Warren searches for any clues that might show them what Mr.
Ruggiero has been hiding.

Warren searches for any clues that might show them what
Mr. Ruggiero has been hiding.
```

INSTRUCTIONS TO YOUR READER

This is both very wrong and a personal pet peeve. Don't speak to the reader as though you are instructing them. Create an experience and allow them to immerse themselves in it, but don't give orders. It's incorrect and unnecessary. Avoid phrases such as

```
We watch as they enter.
We see them drive into the tunnel.
We hear the roar of the jet engines.
We understand the Butler did it.
```

NO!

That the reader knows, sees, hears, or understands should be self-evident. You shouldn't need to offer instructions.

If the Butler did do it and you've done your job to make that clear to the reader, audience, and/or one or more characters within the story, telling the reader what they should realize or understand shouldn't be necessary. Let your visual storytelling do its job. No we watch as they enter. If they're entering on screen, we'll be watching and won't need your instruction to do so. Just say:

```
They enter.
They drive into the tunnel.
The jet engines ROAR.
The Butler did it!
```

As stated previously, you should NOT indicate camera angles or shots as this is not your job, but there will be instances when a close up is required such as on a note left for someone or as someone reads an email on a computer screen.

```
INT. HOTEL SUITE - MORNING

Jack stirs in the bed. His arm reaches out to the
empty space beside him. His eyes open and he sees a
note resting on the pillow.

The Note Reads: What a night! Thanks. You rock, Diane
```

It will be obvious to anyone reading this scene that the contents of the note should be clear and evident on screen and therefore necessitate a close angle. It need not be stated more clearly.

TELEPHONE CONVERSATIONS

This is another common situation where slugging each scene as you move back and forth between two or more parties is unnecessary and becomes very annoying, not to mention a ridiculous waste of your limited pages. The solution is to use INTERCUT.

Introduce each location with its own scene slug, then write INTERCUT AS NEEDED or BEGIN INTERCUT, left-justified and capitalized. At the end of the conversation, write END INTERCUT.

This limits unnecessary scene headings and makes it clear to a reader what is happening. It also allows a director freedom to determine how they will visually execute the scene and what imagery is best. See the example...

As before with the scene involving interior and exterior locations, you'll note how much time and space is saved by not including

```
INT. HOTEL SUITE - LATE NIGHT

Jack can't sleep. Tired of fighting it, he picks up
the phone and DIALS the hotel operator.


INT. HOTEL LOBBY - CONTINUOUS

DIANE, the lone employee working, drops her crossword
and answers the phone.

                    DIANE
              Good evening, Mr. Mellen, how
              may I provide excellent service
              for you?

BEGIN INTERCUT

                    JACK
              I was actually hoping we could
              just talk.

                    DIANE
              I'm not sure I understand sir.

                    JACK
              Well, we're both two kids,
              livin' in the heartland.

                    DIANE
              I'm sorry sir, but I'm not that
              kind of girl.

                    JACK
              Excuse me?

                    DIANE
              Peanut butter and jelly.

                    JACK
              What did you just say?

END INTERCUT

The line goes dead.

Jack looks at his phone, unsure what just happened.
```

scene headings and extra description for every back and forth through the conversation.

The telephone INTERCUT is heavily used and very common so be sure to note how it is employed. It's something that will certainly wind up in your writing sooner rather than later.

FLASHBACKS AND DREAM SEQUENCES

These are handled similarly to the Intercut. Write a scene as you normally would. When a flashback or dream begins, write BEGIN FLASHBACK or BEGIN DREAM, left-justified and capitalized like a scene heading. When it is over, write END FLASHBACK or END DREAM.

Think of this like bookends to mark where the flashback or dream starts and concludes. This way, you can have multiple locations and/or imagery as part of them, but the reader can better see when the dream ends and reality returns. Otherwise, it can be confusing, and that is what you are most trying to avoid.

Here is an example:

Bernard sits in his car, stuck in traffic. A song
comes on the radio and he shudders. His hand goes to
turn it off, but he can't. Tears fill his eyes.

                                                CUT TO:

BEGIN FLASHBACK

INT. GYMNASIUM - NIGHT

A high school prom. Young couples dancing, talking and
having fun. One song ends and a slow one begins. It's
the same one playing in Bernard's car.

A couple dances as three boys sneak up on the boy, who
pulls back slightly and looks at his date's face.

                    BERNARD
          This is the best night of my
          life!

Just then, the three boys pants him from behind and
young Bernard is left standing in his yellow Spongebob
underwear in front of everyone, including his date.

Kids begin laughing. Bernard flushes red and tries to
run away, but his pants around his ankles trips him
and he falls to the ground, making it all much worse.

As he pulls up his pants amidst the laughter, he locks
eyes with his date who isn't laughing, but appears
embarrassed and hurries away.

The sound of a car HONKING!

END FLASHBACK

INT. BERNARD'S CAR - DAY

Bernard snaps out of it as the car behind is honking
for him to move forward.

MONTAGE AND SERIES OF SHOTS

These are popular techniques employing multiple images in quick succession that convey both a passage of time and a progression of action for one or more characters.

Some classic examples would be the training sequence in *Rocky*, the dating montage in *The Naked Gun*, Jennifer Grey learning the dance routine in *Dirty Dancing*, and the burgeoning success of the Ghostbusters as they become household names in NYC. A couple other good ones are Ralph Macchio moving through the early rounds of the competition in *The Karate Kid* and the growing success of Tony Montana's drug empire in *Scarface*.

One key element of a montage is there is typically no dialogue. Most montages are set to a song or piece of music such as "Eye of the Tiger" in *Rocky III* or the opening montage of *Top Gun*, set to Kenny Loggins' "Danger Zone." The major difference between a montage and a series of shots is the level of detail. In a montage, very little needs to be specified whereas with a series of shots, a more detailed list of each image is provided.

A montage provides greater freedom to the director and generally takes less space in a script, while a series of shots expressly states what each image is and therefore makes it squarely the screenwriter's vision.

This is how the opening montage in *Top Gun* might have been written:

```
BEGIN MONTAGE

F-14 Tomcat descends to the carrier deck, its tailhook
snagging the trap wire.

Rapid shots of other fighter planes. Day and night
landings. Sailors on the deck, launching jets into the
air. It's intense, but fun. Speed and adrenaline. A
pilot snaps a salute before takeoff.

END MONTAGE
```

You'll notice, there's quite a bit of freedom to actually shoot this sequence. It's about conveying a theme or emotion. In this case, excitement and adrenaline.

If it is your choice to specifically dictate what shots are included, you can use Series of Shots instead, but be aware this is far less common. Series of Shots will usually take up a lot more space, depending obviously on the number of shots, but you should try to make the description of each image as succinct as possible.

```
BEGIN SERIES OF SHOTS

Describe image #1
Describe image #2
Describe image #3
Describe image #4

END SERIES OF SHOTS
```

Text on Screen

We often see perhaps the name of a city, a year, a quote, or a biblical verse on screen. The way to do this is with SUPER:, which is short for superimpose and on display in the following examples from *Braveheart* and *The Breakfast Club*.

```
EXT. SCOTTISH HIGHLANDS

Various images of the beautiful, but rugged country.

SUPER:     SCOTLAND 1280 A.D.


BLACK SCREEN

SUPER:     "…And these children that you spit on as they try
           to change their worlds are immune to your
           consultations. They're quite aware of what
           they're going through…"

                                            - David Bowie
```

STYLE OF MUSIC

Though it was previously stated you should not identify actual songs in your script, you absolutely can and should identify styles if you deem it important.

The type of music can have a tremendous effect on the tone of any scene or film so while you shouldn't say SMELLS LIKE TEEN SPIRIT plays on the radio, feel free to write that 90s ALT ROCK is blasting or CLASSIC R&B wakes up the crowd and gets them dancing. If you want COUNTRY, say so. You may not get your first choice of artist, but that's not nearly as important.

SPLIT SCREENS

These are not particularly common in modern cinema, though in recent years, it has felt like they are making a bit of a comeback. Just as it sounds, a split screen effect is when you indicate in the script that at least two images and/or scenes are viewed at the same time. Often, this is accomplished simply with a border down the middle of the screen with one scene on either side or on top and bottom. This was often the case in the 1960s, such as in the Rock Hudson/Doris Day films like *Pillow Talk*.

A split screen was famously employed in the late 50s in the film *Indiscreet*, starring Cary Grant and Ingrid Bergman. It was used to get around the censors of that time who objected to showing Grant and Bergman in bed together. Times have certainly changed! Using the split screen, they were each shown on either side of their own beds, talking on the telephone, but with the images next to one another, it appeared as though they were lying together.

More recently, split screens have appeared in Tarantino films like *Kill Bill* and *Jackie Brown*, others like *(500) Days of Summer* and *127 Hours*, as well as in several comic book adaptations.

If you wish to use a split screen, execute it like INTERCUT or FLASHBACK. Introduce a scene, then slug BEGIN SPLIT SCREEN before introducing the additional scene or scenes that will share the screen. Slug END SPLIT SCREEN when you wish for the effect to end and return to a single image.

Fight Scenes

What is the appropriate amount of detail for things like fights scenes, car chases, cooking a turkey, etc.? You obviously want to provide details that make it both exciting and differentiate it from the many other similar scenes people have seen in the past.

My basic rule of thumb is that it gets extremely boring and tedious to read sequences that include every turn of the wheel, every punch or ingredient. In a chase, fast turns shift the action from one street to the next in rapid succession. The reader won't need to retrace the route to find a lost key or something so to tell them every right and left is a laborious waste of space. The same applies to a fight scene. There are going to be punches thrown back and forth. We've all seen enough fight scenes to know that, so detailing every uppercut, sword swipe, and gunshot will get very old very fast. The last thing you want is for it to take twice as long to read the scene as it would to watch it!

So what's the answer? Focus on two things.

First, what makes your chase or your fight different than the others I've already seen? Is it the location? The weaponry? The tactics? What sets your scene apart? Whatever the answer is, that must be featured in the description. For example, a samurai and a Viking happen to bump into one another. The language barrier causes instant chaos and out comes the sword and axe...

Second, what are the key moments, as they are what you should feature in your writing? How does the fight or chase begin or conclude? With any of these types of scenes, there are pivotal beats that dictate the outcome. A lucky shot to the jaw, someone crossing the street and forcing a car off the road, etc.

When and how does one character get the upper hand over the other? The elements that determine the result of the fight scene, car chase, or similar event are ultimately the only ones a reader needs to see.

WRITING EXERCISE:
No Interior Designers!

An excellent way to practice effective description for a screenplay is to hone your ability to set a scene with brevity.

Describe the following 20 locations using no more than 3 lines and by lines, I don't mean sentences — I MEAN LINES!

1. Oscar Piddle's Taxidermy Shop
2. The In-Laws' New Condo
3. US Customs Warehouse
4. Cheap Motel Room
5. Isabella's Kitchen
6. A Prison Drunk Tank
7. Mrs. Hack's First Grade Classroom
8. Doctor Patel's Office
9. Hannibal Lecter's Childhood Bedroom
10. Laverne's Beauty Salon
11. Traffic Court
12. The Goodyear Blimp Hangar
13. Department Store Fitting Room
14. Private Ridley's Foxhole
15. The Bottoms Up Lounge
16. Six Flags Amusement Park Restroom
17. Airport First-Class Lounge
18. Child's Secret Place
19. One of the original 7 Wonders of the World
20. Poolside Cabana

Take note of the fact that I avoided specifying geographic locations. Traffic court in Jackson Hole, Wyoming likely looks different than in Detroit or Maui. A poolside cabana in Vegas is not at all like the one at my friend Roy's house. Again, what differentiates the specific location, and what is notable that a reader should be aware of?

CHARACTER SLUGS

The third element of a scene. Character slugs are ALWAYS CAPITALIZED even if it's not a proper name such as DOCTOR or CRAZY LADY. **Be consistent.** If you use the slug LUKE in the beginning, don't switch to SKYWALKER later as it gets confusing.

One variation on this is if one character uses a nickname for another. Let's say someone calls TED JONES, "TJ." In that case, the nickname would appear in the dialogue, but you would still refer to the character as TED in both description and when doing his character slug.

```
                    BOBBY
          Hey, TJ... What's up?

  Ted turns around and sees Bobby approaching.

                    TED
          Just living the dream, how
          about you?
```

However, be aware that if everyone calls him TJ, then that should probably be used for all elements.

Use one name and no titles for your main characters. So DETECTIVE MARTIN RIGGS should not be DETECTIVE MARTIN RIGGS, MARTIN RIGGS, or DET. RIGGS. He should just be MARTIN or RIGGS, and since that character in *Lethal Weapon* generally goes by Riggs, that's the slug... RIGGS.

Less prominent characters with titles such as Officer, Reverend, Principal, Admiral, and so forth, should be slugged with their titles as it is helpful in differentiating them and keeping track of the function they serve. DR. JONES, RABBI LEVY, PRINCE DUDLEY, etc....

You may have a character that is in just one or two scenes and not important, beyond the job they do, such as a doctor, police officer, waiter, or king. In this case, use ONLY the title as it indicates to the reader to be aware of the function more so than their personality.

Some examples include COP, BARTENDER, DOG CATCHER, or HEALTH INSPECTOR.

There will be times when a character's name will change during the story because an alias or alternate identity is revealed. Perhaps you have a character that speaks as two people like BATMAN and BRUCE WAYNE. There may also be a case where a character is initially anonymous, perhaps slugged as VAGRANT or STALKER only to later be given an actual name. Since your reader is hopefully experiencing the screenplay as an audience would in a theater, don't give the surprise away by prematurely announcing a secret identity. Simply slug the first name or title normally and when the secret is revealed, slug it once as VAGRANT/RALPH or STALKER/VINCE, then continue with the new name as the slug: RALPH or VINCE.

```
     Rachel walks towards the coffee shop and as usual, the
     same vagrant is pan handling out front.

     When she approaches the door, he opens it for her with
     a bright smile.

                         RACHEL
               You open the door for me every
               morning. Thank you.

                         VAGRANT
               Happy to help.

                         RACHEL
               What's your name?

                         VAGRANT/RALPH
               It's Ralph. Thanks for asking.

                         RACHEL
               Would you like a coffee, Ralph?

                         RALPH
               I'd love some!
```

In the case of BATMAN and BRUCE WAYNE, who go back and forth, speaking as both characters, you slug them as the character they are in a particular scene. It's unlikely that they will both be in the same scene, but if that happens, it simply depends on whether the audience or reader is already aware of the double identity or not. If they are not aware, follow the rule as before. Start as BATMAN and after the switch, slug it once as BATMAN/BRUCE, then continue as BRUCE. If they are aware, skip the middle step and just make the switch to BRUCE.

CHARACTER SLUG EXTENSIONS

These are provided in parentheses ( ) to identify where a voice is coming from when the character is NOT visible on screen. Once again, this is something that screenwriting software will help you with. The extension goes on the same line as the Slug, separated by a single space. Common extensions include:

(V.O.)	Voice Over, like a narrator
(O.S.)	Off Screen, such as screaming from another room
(O.C.)	Off Camera, likely in the same room or area, but not in the shot
(ON TV)	The words spoken by someone on television, such as a news anchor
(RADIO)	Words coming via a radio
(ON SCREEN)	Words spoken on a movie or computer screen

```
                    REX (O.S.)
              Come upstairs! You've got to
              see this.

Or...

                    ETHAN (O.C.)
              What are you thinking?

     Summer turns, revealing Ethan who is across the room.

                    SUMMER
              I don't trust him.
```

Another common extension is (cont'd). It's placed after a character slug when dialogue is broken up by description, but the same person continues speaking uninterrupted by another character. Screenwriting software will place it for you.

```
                      REX (O.S.)
                Come upstairs! Hurry.

     Eve doesn't respond. She continues to slice her apple.

     A moment passes before Rex appears.

                      REX (cont'd)
                Didn't you hear me calling you?
```

DIALOGUE

The fourth element of a scene. In Chapter 8, the content of dialogue was discussed in great detail. This section is about the execution of dialogue.

The first thing to note is that regardless of the length, dialogue should be one uninterrupted block of words, phrases, and sentences. DO NOT separate dialogue into different paragraphs. It should read the same way it would be spoken by the actors. Keep in mind people tend not to speak in lengthy blocks so you should look to break up long speeches with action on screen. In the case that someone is giving a speech or perhaps delivering a eulogy, you should still find ways to break it up such as describing activity in the crowd. It can be as simple as having the speaker take a sip of water or shift their attention to someone coughing. Anything to break up an especially long block of dialogue will make it easier to read and appear more natural.

Though software will typically handle this for you, you should ALWAYS end on a complete sentence. Do not end one page in the middle of a sentence and then pick it up at the top of the next page. Once again, this about avoiding speed bumps. It's much smoother to have a completed thought at the end of a page and then move on to the next page and start fresh. Finish a sentence and place (MORE) centered at the bottom of the page. On the following page, slug the same character with the extension (cont'd) and resume their dialogue.

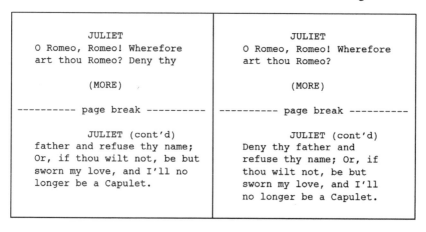

```
          JULIET                          JULIET
O Romeo, Romeo! Wherefore        O Romeo, Romeo! Wherefore
art thou Romeo? Deny thy         art thou Romeo?

        (MORE)                           (MORE)

---------- page break ----------    ---------- page break ----------

      JULIET (cont'd)                JULIET (cont'd)
father and refuse thy name;      Deny thy father and
Or, if thou wilt not, be but     refuse thy name; Or, if
sworn my love, and I'll no       thou wilt not, be but
longer be a Capulet.             sworn my love, and I'll
                                 no longer be a Capulet.
```

PARENTHESES

They can be a useful device with dialogue; however, they are also WILDLY overused, and thus devalued by less experienced screenwriters. This is something you must look out for and be careful to avoid. Parentheses, placed under the character slug, are intended to convey information specifically relevant to the dialogue itself. **How a line should sound or be read.**

This isn't something actors will appreciate if you overuse. As has been said repeatedly, do your job and not someone else's.

A helpful rule of thumb is to only use parentheses when the dialogue is to be delivered in a manner OTHER than what one would expect. In the first example on the next page, between the content of the line and the exclamation point, screaming probably goes without saying. In the second example, the parentheses are warranted because it's an unexpected delivery of the line.

```
                    STEVE
                 (screaming)
          The aliens have landed!


                    STEVE
                  (whispers)
          The aliens have landed!
```

Parentheses are also used when multiple characters are together and one says something not to the group, but to one specific person.

```
     Brandon and Kelley laugh as Dylan approaches with Brenda.

                    BRANDON
                  (to Brenda)
          Have you talked to Dad?
```

In most cases, your dialogue should speak for itself. However, there will be times where you'll want to add a simple piece of instruction for the actor such as (sarcastic), (goofy), (slick), etc.

Another example of overuse with parentheses is the inclusion of a (beat) which is a break in the dialogue that forces a pause while characters consider what's been said or react to something. In most cases, this type of thing doesn't need to be pointed out as once again, your dialogue should indicate the necessity for a break on its own, but sometimes it is important and useful to include. There are also times when you use a (beat) to suggest whomever is speaking pauses to consider or choose their next words carefully or perhaps in the delivery of a joke. People tend to pause before revealing a punch line.

```
                    LARRY
          What do you call a man with
          no arms or legs who gets into
          a fight with his cat?
                    (beat)
          Claude.
```

It's also appropriate if you are only showing one side of a phone conversation. Employ beats to suggest the character is listening to what the person on the other end of the line is saying.

```
                    STINKY JONES
                    (on phone)
        I know it's late, but I swear
        you'll have it.
                    (beat)
        Just one more day. I'm begging
        you!
                    (beat)
        You won't regret it.
```

A somewhat dicey use of parentheses is to note an action, such as above where it indicates the character is speaking on the telephone. Technically, the parentheses are only supposed to relate to the delivery of the dialogue, but in a case such as this, it's short and compact and thus allows for the scene to move more smoothly than if you broke it up to indicate the same information via description. These are fine (answers phone) (points at Bob) but not...

```
                    JIMMY
                    (screams as he pulls
                    into the parking lot
                    and stops in front of
                    her)
        What's up?
```

You can see how absurd it looks and reads when you incorrectly use parentheses to note more extensive action.

The helpful rule to follow is that if you can't say it in 2 or 3 words, it probably doesn't belong inside parentheses, but rather in description.

NUMBERS

If it does NOT matter to you as the writer how a character speaks a number, simply write the number, such as 262. However, if it is important, you need to spell it out. 262 could be two six two or two hundred sixty-two or two sixty-two, and you need to be specific in such a case.

Years are generally said the same way by everybody so most of the time you will simply use a number such as 2063 or 1812. However, in the case that you want a character to say twenty ought ten rather than 2010, you need to spell that out.

DIALECTS, ACCENTS, FOREIGN LANGUAGES, AND SUBTITLES

These are all common in screenwriting. The first thing is: DO NOT write dialogue phonetically to represent someone with a thick accent or who speaks broken English. It gets very confusing and slows the read as the only way to understand what you've written is to actually sound out the words. It is fine to mix in a few colloquialisms, such as "gimme," "ya'll," "bloke," or "howdy" as those are about character, personality, and maybe an accent, but the bulk of the dialogue should otherwise appear normal.

You can also use parentheses under a character slug and say (Southern accent). If the character speaks a great deal, you don't want to keep repeating this so instead, say in the description:

Savannah speaks with a Southern accent.

Now the reader has that knowledge through all forthcoming scenes where she speaks.

DO NOT write blocks of dialogue in another language, even if that's how it's to be delivered in the movie. The reader isn't likely to understand it and that's more important. State in the description that the following lines are in Dutch or Japanese or Swahili and then write the dialogue in English.

The exception is if you are just talking about a line or two and/ or the meaning will be clear even to someone who doesn't speak the language. For example:

```
Carl pulls into a gas station. He gets out of the car
and approaches a mechanic.

                    CARL
          Excuse me, can you tell me how
          to find the highway?

                  MECHANIC
          No comprende, Senor.
```

You don't need to understand Spanish to get this and the effort of doing it another way is likely more trouble than it's worth.

If you have a character speaking Dutch and you want them to speak Dutch with subtitles, you would simply write that in the description before their dialogue begins. You might also use a parenthetical (in Dutch) under a character slug depending on how substantial the part is and then you would write their actual dialogue in English.

If a whole conversation occurs in Japanese through an entire scene, you should write the dialogue in English, but in the description at the beginning, you would indicate on a separate line:

The dialogue is in Japanese with English subtitles.

You also have the option of including, depending on the length of the scene and whether you feel it's necessary for the sake of clarity or not, BEGIN SUBTITLES and END SUBTITLES like you would INTERCUT, MONTAGE, or FLASHBACK.

DO NOT include both the English and foreign language versions side by side or one over the other. It doubles the space you are using, creates confusion, and slows the read, while also being entirely unnecessary.

SINGING, QUOTING, READING, RECITING...

There will be times when characters sing, recite poems or lyrics, quote JFK, or read from a newspaper. In each case, the words are written as normal dialogue, but they should be inside quotation marks to demonstrate they are different from normal speech. Additionally, indicate via description, a parenthetical, or both, any further information to clarify the situation. For example, if someone were reading aloud from *A Christmas Carol*, you would indicate in the description that they are holding Dickens' *A Christmas Carol* or they might say via dialogue what they are about to read. You would also use a parenthetical like (reading).

If someone sings a line from "Viva Las Vegas," you would include a parenthetical that says (singing), then write the line as dialogue and in quotations. There should rarely be a case where you would write out the lyrics to an entire song so keep it to what's vital for the scene. If the whole song is going to be performed, you would indicate that via description. Similarly, you would handle speeches or other recitations such as reading news copy or from a webpage in much the same manner.

DOUBLE DASH AND ELLIPSIS...

People's dialogue is often interrupted by a host of issues from other characters to loud noises, to perhaps a sneeze. They typically don't speak in complete sentences to begin with. They cough or stutter, forget what they were going to say, or struggle to get their words out. Sometimes they can't pronounce a word correctly and keep trying and other times they're distracted by a person or action that pulls their attention away.

I cannot recommend enough that you practice and gain proficiency with double dashes and ellipses. They are an indicator of more advanced screenwriting technique and will improve the quality of your dialogue and its readability. Moreover, it will make your dialogue sound more realistic.

THE DOUBLE DASH -- is commonly used to indicate when dialogue is interrupted. This is also the method to use when dialogue resumes, mid-sentence, placing it before the dialogue, rather than after.

```
                    TIMMY
          Mom, I just want to watch
          for ten more --

                    MOM
          I don't want to hear it,
          Timmy. It's bedtime.

                    TIMMY
                  (mumbles)
          -- unfair.

                    MOM
          What was that?

Or...

      Stella hurries up the stairs, turns the corner and
      opens Michael's door without knocking.

                    MICHAEL
                  (on phone)
          -- talking to me and said
          better late than --
                  (to Stella)
          Could you knock maybe?!
```

ELLIPSES... are primarily used when dialogue trails off or someone stops speaking in mid-sentence. They are used when a character is leading someone else with their dialogue and are common to flashbacks and dreams as well.

```
          Grandpa sits on the edge of the bed. He cracks open
          the book and begins.

                              GRANDPA
                            (reading)
                    Once upon a time...

Or...

                              LANCE
                    So I was thinking it's time
                    we get back together. I swear,
                    I'll never look at another
                    woman again. I just don't want
                    to live another day...

          Suddenly, his gaze shifts to a curvy redhead passing
          their table.

                              KIM
                    Yeah, right. You jerk!
```

OVERLAPPING CONVERSATIONS

It's rare, but occasionally writers want more than one conversation to be going on at the same time with both being prominent. That is to say, neither is relegated strictly to the background as just noise. This is an uncommon scenario. You might have different conversations at a party for example, but you wouldn't include all of the dialogue from multiple conversations at the same time. When you do want two conversations to overlap, do not place separate dialogue blocks side by side. Just because it looks right, people can't read two things at once. It's confusing and it breaks up the flow.

Instead, break up the dialogue into fragments and alternate with a parenthetical that says (overlapping). Use double dashes to help indicate the switch back and forth.

The above conversation might look like this:

```
EXT. BOX OFFICE - AFTERNOON

A man and woman each wait separately in line to buy
tickets. Both are speaking on their cell phones.

                    MAN
                (on phone)
            I told you honey, I'll
            pick the dog up from the
            groomer when I'm done here.

                    WOMAN
                (overlapping)
            I can't wait to see you
            later.

                    MAN
            -- supposed to do that if
            I'm picking up Mr.
            Fluffernutter? --

                    WOMAN
            Are you kidding, of course
            we can listen to Celine Dion
            all night long. That's how you
            know it's a party!

                    MAN
            -- really don't care. I'll
            get the dog, you get the
            mustard! --
```

TRANSITIONS

The fifth and final element of a scene. Their purpose is to help clarify to a reader that you are shifting from one location to another and from one sequence to the next. They also indicate HOW to visually move from one scene to another; however, as moving beyond a simple CUT creeps into a director's territory, some of the more exotic transitions should be avoided.

The use of transitions is a practiced skill. DO NOT include them between every scene, as it will only add unnecessary bulk to your script and that space is better devoted to your story and characters. It also becomes a distraction to the reader. The opposite is also true in that there are absolutely times when a transition is instrumental in showing that a long sequence has ended and the focus is shifting.

In spec screenwriting, the best use of transitions is between sequences, not scenes. This means that while you follow one or more characters, possibly through multiple locations or through different rooms in one larger location, a transition is NOT necessary. When you do cut to a new location, a new set of characters, or the time has shifted in any direction, a transition assists the reader to follow your storytelling. Whereas overuse can be distracting and unnecessary, the proper implementation of transitions is very helpful and an indication of professional screenwriting.

So, for example, let's say that KYLE is sitting in a high school classroom when the bell rings. You've set the scene and now he rises and exits into the hallway, goes through some doors into a second hallway and then down some stairs to the boy's locker room. You would NOT need to put transitions and new scene headings in for each location. It's one sequence within a larger location that the reader is aware of from description. If instead of going into the locker room, he exits the building and goes to his car in the parking lot, you **would** need a new scene heading to indicate the action has moved to an exterior location, but you still would NOT need a transition. Think of it visually. It's a seamless action. However, if upon entering the locker room, the scene shifts to Kyle's mother, a doctor performing surgery in a hospital operating room, CUT TO: helps the reader recognize the shifting perspective. It lets them know the story has moved to a new place and a new character.

You are familiar with FADE IN: and FADE OUT: which will appear at the beginning and end of your script, respectively. The only other transition you need is CUT TO:. There just simply isn't a need for the others during the spec phase. They are options within screenwriting software because it caters to screenwriters and directors working in other stages of the process as well.

Dissolves, smash cuts, iris in, wipes, and so forth are simply not your territory.

At the completion of a scene, the transition is placed, flushed against the right margin, in ALL CAPS with a colon as follows...

CUT TO:

QUICK REMINDER...
THE FIVE ELEMENTS OF A SCENE

1. Scene Headings aka Scene Slugs
2. Description aka Action
3. Character Slugs
4. Dialogue
5. Transitions

KEYS TO REMEMBER

- There are always exceptions, but generally speaking, remember that less is more. Extra words, thoughts, phrases, gestures, movements, and actions often bring little more to your screenplay other than additional pages. Your goal with a spec script, particularly if you've never sold one before, is to engage and amaze as quickly and efficiently as possible because the odds are most industry professionals won't be enticed by your work otherwise.

- Recognize those moments where it is not only unnecessary to use a new scene heading for every new location, such as the rooms of a house, but also that doing so will drastically and noticeably stall the pacing and flow of your script.

- When it comes to description, be a screenwriter, not an interior designer! In other writing mediums, you are encouraged to paint a vibrant picture for the reader; but in screenwriting, you will literally have a vibrant picture. Therefore, unnecessarily dense description on the page is often a wasted and misguided effort.

- The more characters you introduce by name, the more confusing it gets. Use titles and functions for characters that need not be remembered with great clarity.

- Consistency is important because it contributes to a smooth read. The way you list ages, the names by which you refer to recurring characters or locations in description and Character Slugs are all examples of elements that must remain consistent throughout a script to avoid confusion.

- Write visually. If I can't see what you've written on screen, it doesn't belong in a screenplay.

- Used sparingly, parentheses bring value, but being employed improperly or used too often has the opposite effect.

- Do not write in a foreign language. No one is impressed that you can write in Mandarin or Portuguese. It just looks like pages of nonsense.

- Don't get cute with transitions. CUT TO: is really the only one you should need in a spec script. Using a bunch of others is typically a clear signal that the writer is both pretentious and new to the craft.

FINAL THOUGHTS...

I considered including an additional chapter in this book on the business of screenwriting. Ultimately, I decided against it because it felt like putting the cart before the horse. You need to learn HOW to write a professional screenplay before you plot the advancement of your Hollywood career. Otherwise, it's like deciding how you intend to spend your lottery millions before you've actually hit the jackpot... a fun exercise, but not exactly practical. Now that being said, I did want to make a few important points as they impact on your content and execution.

First, bear in mind that there is a significant difference between the art or craft of screenwriting and the business of screenwriting, and while the latter certainly requires literary artistry and talent, the former can most definitely exist without financial reward and quite frequently does. You must decide if you are truly seeking to make this your career, and if so, here are a few things to consider.

The Writers Guild minimums for a completed original script, which change periodically as union contracts are renegotiated, are approximately $50,000 for low budget and $100,000 for high. Production budgets, particularly at the studio level, will typically be in the millions, if not tens or even hundreds of millions of dollars. Think about that sum of money. The budget for an inexpensive studio film is significantly more money than most individuals will see in their entire lifetime.

So why is this important? For starters, if your script is actually chosen to become a film, it is now a global product... a commodity that must be marketed and sold to millions of people for its financial backers to see a positive return on their investment. The stakes are outrageously high, necessitating decisions that go well beyond whether a scene or even an entire script is well written or boasts an intriguing or original voice. It's just not that simple and to believe it is means you are operating with childlike blinders on. This is the major leagues — only adults may participate.

With that much money on the line, there will be several people whose job it is to safeguard that investment by utilizing their experience to shape your script into a film that audiences will pay to see. You need to be prepared for lots of cooks invading your kitchen. You've made the dough, but what it will become is often out of your hands. Sometimes, the process is a success and a fantastic film emerges; other times, the effort fails and corporate stock prices can drop as a result. It's a screenplay for you and however important it may be, people lose their jobs and sometimes their careers over bad decisions that culminate in underperforming box office. Like I said, the major leagues!

To achieve true commercial success, your concept, regardless of genre, MUST be appealing to an audience that goes well beyond you and yours. Your execution MUST be superior to 99% of the other scripts out there. You MUST be open to notes and changes and receptive to your work being one piece, albeit a crucial one, to an immense collaboration that will include many other voices, ideas, interpretations, and agendas.

For those of you who watched one or more lousy movies and said to yourself some version of "How the hell did that junk get made?" and/or "I could've written something so much better!" — get over it because life and Hollywood aren't that black and white. Professionals don't set out to make bad movies. They can happen for a host of reasons, only one of which is a poor script. The salient point is that more often than not, Hollywood is predisposed to go with what it knows. That means writers and other professionals that have delivered in the past and have a track record of success because the powers that be don't know you exist, even if your voice is the one they so desperately need. If you want that to change, you are going to have to work incredibly hard and fight to get their attention. It is a battle well worth waging, especially if you have the drive and talent to succeed as victory does indeed come with great rewards.

Don't be in too much of a rush. I know that's very easy to say, but completing a script on a schedule isn't likely to generate something that's better than 99% of the other scripts out there. Established screen-writers often have deadlines because they are working for a studio and other considerations like an actor's availability, the duration of an option, or a release schedule may contribute to that being necessary, but remember, this is about writing spec scripts, not working on assign-ment which is a level of success you have not likely achieved as of yet. Go ahead and force yourself to write every day or devote X number of hours per week to the script. Maybe even have a rough idea of when you'd like to finish, but far too often, less experienced screenwriters are in such a hurry to move on from the actual writing phase that they do so to the detriment of the work. It's ready when it's ready and not a minute sooner.

A word of caution. So many aspiring screenwriters get into this because they have one story to tell. It's often a true story and very personal to the author.

It can't be emphasized enough how unlikely it is that your first script will be a success. Great writing comes with practice and with its unique blend of elements, screenwriting often requires more than most other forms. You aren't likely to do that single passion project justice if you are learning how to write a screenplay at the same time you are trying to tell what is often a very execution dependent, character driven, and nuanced story. If you are serious, you'll consider practicing on another idea first. Finally, while many who are new to this have one story to tell, professional screenwriters are typically overflowing with ideas and a desire to write them all. This is something to strongly consider if you fall into the first category and are just thinking you can dip your toes in the water and find success both easily and quickly. In either case, best of luck to all of you as you endeavor to make your particular screenwriting dreams a reality.

CHAPTER 14

Bonus Writing Exercises...
Practice Makes Perfect

WRITING EXERCISE: THEM'S FIGHTIN' WORDS

Time to write an argument. This exercise will give you practice with both the content and execution of dialogue.

Conflict is a necessary component of quality screenwriting. Characters can't always be on the same page, even if they are allies.

Write a scene with your protagonist engaged in an argument with a supporting character who is NOT the antagonist... That's too easy.

The disagreement should be between allies or friends, not rivals on opposing sides of a larger fight.

As people are even less likely to speak in complete sentences and with proper grammar during an argument, make use of the ellipsis (...), double dash (--), and (parentheses). Include interruptions, maybe some overlapping talk as they attempt to speak over one another, yelling and using body language, etc....

Take some time to get a sense of both character's personalities because distinct voice should always be on your mind whenever you are working on dialogue.

Try also to reveal something about each of the characters. When people engage in arguments and lose their tempers, they tend to say things they don't mean, reveal things they didn't intend to, and quite often show a more honest portrayal of their true character. Take advantage of that.

WRITING EXERCISE: WHAT AM I SEEING?

Screenwriting is a visual medium, meant to be watched, not read. As screenwriters, you have a difficult challenge. You must write something that reads clearly and is engaging, but is nevertheless a blueprint for a visual experience. This exercise will help you practice the skill of show me, don't tell me.

Description identifies what's on screen. When you write emotions, thoughts, and/or feelings without including any method by which they are clear and evident to the audience, you are writing a novel, not a script.

How would you describe these visually, without overtly stating it in dialogue?

1. Dante fears his past will come back to haunt him.
2. Sheila is hopelessly in love with Raj.
3. Detective Brewster is irate at being lied to by the suspect.
4. The sun is shining much brighter around the corner.
5. Wallace can't stop thinking about what to buy first.
6. Carl is jealous of Fred's relationship with Stephanie.
7. Isaac is convinced Wendy is lying.
8. Julius is optimistic about tomorrow.
9. Sam's nervous about her upcoming surgery.
10. Timmy wants his mommy.

How can you describe these moments so that an audience can see them? How are these things expressed visually?

You don't need to write actual scenes, though you certainly can and it would be great practice. But try to write the description and see if you can't devise a few alternatives for each.

Mastery of this skill is a key difference between writing a story and scripting a film.

WRITING EXERCISE: Make an Impression!

A successful, PROFESSIONAL screenwriter goes beyond the content of their own writing and has an understanding of the business of motion pictures. You can't expect to write something that a multinational company will spend tens of millions of dollars on and be completely oblivious about sales, marketing, and distribution.

That is simply unrealistic and incredibly naïve. One way to help with this is to make you think like a marketing executive. It's time to devise a new title for your latest script.

A few things to consider…

- It's a sales pitch as much if not more than an artistic statement. Be clear and evocative, not obscure and confusing. You are not trying to trick or deceive an audience, but to tempt and engage their interest.
- Your title should indicate elements of genre. As an example, *The Purge* sounds like a horror film and *Wedding Crashers* a comedy. I wouldn't expect *Armageddon* to be a drama, would you?
- Your title should also indicate elements of plot and/or your central conflict, without giving away the resolution. Take *Fatal Attraction*, as an example.

Start by making a list of words that either describe your plot, the driving tone or emotion of the film, or the protagonist. Use a thesaurus!

For each word on your list, pair it with three different adjectives that reflect the tone of your script.

So a horror film might get pairs like Frozen Fear, Deranged Masquerade, or Rabid Death. A comedy might see The Flatulent Four, Sweaty Revenge, or Bodacious Banditos.

Also consider single, descriptive words such as *Taken, Vertigo, Jaws, Big,* and *Fargo*.

Have some fun and sell your movie!

WRITING EXERCISE: THE MANIPULATION

This is an exercise designed to enhance your skill with both dialogue and character. As the goal is subtlety and nuance, the better your scene is, the more advanced your writing has become.

Write a scene with one character attempting to manipulate another into either providing a piece of information or agreeing to do something they normally would not.

Maybe it's an attempt at seduction or perhaps a parent needs their child to stop playing and go to bed. It could be a spy trying to turn a foreign operative or one sibling working to get their brother or sister to take the blame for a misdeed of some sort.

Assuming the manipulator will be successful in their efforts, I recommend you make them work for it. Don't let it be easy as that will defeat the purpose of the exercise.

Make use of subtext and write visually as painting a picture of the stakes or future consequences of not cooperating will often be part of a successful manipulation.

Remember that dialogue is often more interesting if it becomes animated or is tainted with emotion, such as anger or insecurity.

If there is an applicable situation in your own story, feel free to use this exercise to improve your execution of that scene.

Now get to work... You know you want to... Come on, it'll be fun...

WRITING EXERCISE: Before & After

The goal of this exercise is to work on the evolution of character. As has been discussed, your characters must evolve over the course of your story. They must be affected in some manner by the challenges they face, the obstacles they overcome, and the failures that set them back. How does that change become evident to your audience? How do you gradually show that evolution from moment to moment?

You will write two scenes, which as the title suggests, are before and after an important event. They will feature a protagonist talking to the same person in both scenes. Try not to use dialogue as a crutch to convey everything the character is thinking or feeling.

Employ subtext and be visual in your description.

Some options...
• A Blind Date
• An Interview for a New Job
• Starting at Quarterback in the Super Bowl
• Flying a Bombing Mission During the Vietnam War
• Attending Their Ex-Boyfriend or Girlfriend's Wedding

Feel free to choose an event from your own story if that makes the exercise more helpful.

Begin with a scene featuring the protagonist just prior to the event. They could be getting dressed and talking to a friend or on their way. Don't have them writing a letter as that will just wind up being dialogue that tells the entire story.

Follow that with a second scene sometime after the event. How did it go? What might the audience be able to discern about the emotions of your character based on their behavior? How has the character changed and/or been affected by the experience?

It doesn't have to be harrowing or negative. Evolution in any direction is fine, as long as there is clear and obvious movement.

WRITING EXERCISE: Best Day/Worst Day

This is another character exercise that offers more of an emotional insight into the hearts and minds of your characters that goes beyond what might be included in their bio.

You are going to write a scene featuring one of your main characters. It will likely make the most sense and be most helpful with your protagonist; however it could be equally insightful for your antagonist or a featured supporting character.

Write a scene where your character is being interviewed. It's not really important where or why, only that they are inclined to be honest in their responses. That said, honest doesn't mean they aren't evasive, self-conscious, sarcastic, or anything else that might serve to deflect some of the spotlight or minimize their feelings of exposure.

The interview has only 2 questions…

1. Tell me about the best day of your life.
2. Please describe the worst day of your life.

You must decide if their answers include events from your story or if this interview preceded the time period of the film. Perhaps it is long after, with the character now old.

Their best and worst days could also be the same day.

What they perceive as their best and worst days and how they describe them will add a tremendous amount of depth to their personalities in your script.

About the Author...

A dam was born and raised in
Baltimore, Maryland and moved
to Los Angeles shortly after gradu-
ating from the George Washington
University to pursue a career in film
production. After more than two
decades in the business, his résumé is
a distinctive blend of experience that
makes him uniquely qualified to teach
and discuss screenwriting.

He has been a script reader at a major agency, story editor for
one of the most prolific producers in film history, Vice President
of Development for arguably the most script-conscious and literate
producers of all time, and Vice President of Production for a third
hugely successful producer. He has been a screenwriter, a producer, a
director, as well as a professor, and now adds the title of author to his
varied background.

In his executive positions, just a select few of the films he has
worked on include *Executive Decision, The Matrix, The Truman Show,
In & Out, A Simple Plan, Wonder Boys, I, Robot,* and *Behind Enemy
Lines.* He co-produced *The Express* for Universal, and wrote, produced,
and directed the independent drama *It's Dark Here.*

This diversity of experience means that he has seen screenwriting
from every conceivable angle, including both artistic and professional,
making him an expert worth learning from.

His services as a teacher, consultant, and author are also available
on his website, justscreenwrite.com.

SAVE THE CAT!®
THE LAST BOOK ON SCREENWRITING YOU'LL EVER NEED!

BLAKE SNYDER

BEST SELLER

He's made millions of dollars selling screenplays to Hollywood and now screenwriter Blake Snyder tells all. "Save the Cat!®" is just one of Snyder's many ironclad rules for making your ideas more marketable and your script more satisfying – and saleable, including:

- The four elements of every winning logline.
- The seven immutable laws of screenplay physics.
- The 10 genres and why they're important to your movie.
- Why your Hero must serve your idea.
- Mastering the Beats.
- Mastering the Board to create the Perfect Beast.
- How to get back on track with ironclad and proven rules for script repair.

This ultimate insider's guide reveals the secrets that none dare admit, told by a show biz veteran who's proven that you can sell your script if you can save the cat.

"Imagine what would happen in a town where more writers approached screenwriting the way Blake suggests? My weekend read would dramatically improve, both in sellable/producible content and in discovering new writers who understand the craft of storytelling and can be hired on assignment for ideas we already have in house."
> – From the Foreword by Sheila Hanahan Taylor, Vice President,Development at Zide/Perry Entertainment, whose films include *American Pie, Cats and Dogs, Final Destination*

"One of the most comprehensive and insightful how-to's out there. Save the Cat!® is a must-read for both the novice and the professional screenwriter."
> – Todd Black, Producer, *The Pursuit of Happyness, The Weather Man, S.W.A.T, Alex and Emma, Antwone Fisher*

"Want to know how to be a successful writer in Hollywood? The answers are here. Blake Snyder has written an insider's book that's informative – and funny, too."
> – David Hoberman, Producer, *The Shaggy Dog* (2005), *Raising Helen, Walking Tall, Bringing Down the House, Monk* (TV)

BLAKE SNYDER, besides selling million-dollar scripts to both Disney and Spielberg, was one of Hollywood's most successful spec screenwriters. Blake's vision continues on *www.blakesnyder.com.*

$20.95 · 216 PAGES · ORDER NUMBER 34RLS · ISBN: 9781932907001

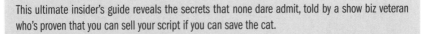

24 HOURS | 1.800.833.5738 | WWW.MWP.COM

THE WRITER'S JOURNEY
3RD EDITION

MYTHIC STRUCTURE FOR WRITERS

CHRISTOPHER VOGLER

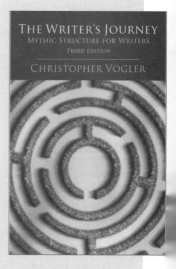

BEST SELLER
OVER 170,000 COPIES SOLD!

See why this book has become an international best seller and a true classic. *The Writer's Journey* explores the powerful relationship between mythology and storytelling in a clear, concise style that's made it required reading for movie executives, screenwriters, playwrights, scholars, and fans of pop culture all over the world.

Both fiction and nonfiction writers will discover a set of useful myth-inspired storytelling paradigms (i.e., "The Hero's Journey") and step-by-step guidelines to plot and character development. Based on the work of Joseph Campbell, *The Writer's Journey* is a must for all writers interested in further developing their craft.

The updated and revised third edition provides new insights and observations from Vogler's ongoing work on mythology's influence on stories, movies, and man himself.

"This book is like having the smartest person in the story meeting come home with you and whisper what to do in your ear as you write a screenplay. Insight for insight, step for step, Chris Vogler takes us through the process of connecting theme to story and making a script come alive."
— Lynda Obst, Producer, *Sleepless in Seattle, How to Lose a Guy in 10 Days;* Author, *Hello, He Lied*

"This is a book about the stories we write, and perhaps more importantly, the stories we live. It is the most influential work I have yet encountered on the art, nature, and the very purpose of storytelling."
— Bruce Joel Rubin, Screenwriter, *Stuart Little 2, Deep Impact, Ghost, Jacob's Ladder*

CHRISTOPHER VOGLER is a veteran story consultant for major Hollywood film companies and a respected teacher of filmmakers and writers around the globe. He has influenced the stories of movies from *The Lion King* to *Fight Club* to *The Thin Red Line* and most recently wrote the first installment of *Ravenskull*, a Japanese-style manga or graphic novel. He is the executive producer of the feature film *P.S. Your Cat is Dead* and writer of the animated feature *Jester Till.*

$27.95 · 300 PAGES · ORDER NUMBER 76RLS · ISBN: 193290736x

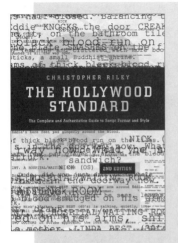

THE HOLLYWOOD STANDARD
2ND EDITION
THE COMPLETE AND AUTHORITATIVE GUIDE TO SCRIPT FORMAT AND STYLE

CHRISTOPHER RILEY

This is the book screenwriter Antwone Fisher (*Antwone Fisher*, *Tales from the Script*) insists his writing students at UCLA read. This book convinced John August (*Big Fish*, *Charlie and the Chocolate Factory*) to stop dispensing formatting advice on his popular writing website. His new advice: Consult *The Hollywood Standard*. The book working and aspiring writers keep beside their keyboards and rely on every day. Written by a professional screenwriter whose day job was running the vaunted script shop at Warner Bros., this book is used at USC's School of Cinema, UCLA, and the acclaimed Act One Writing Program in Hollywood, and in screenwriting programs around the world. It is the definitive guide to script format.

The Hollywood Standard describes in clear, vivid prose and hundreds of examples how to format every element of a screenplay or television script. A reference for everyone who writes for the screen, from the novice to the veteran, this is the dictionary of script format, with instructions for formatting everything from the simplest master scene heading to the most complex and challenging musical underwater dream sequence. This new edition includes a quick start guide, plus new chapters on avoiding a dozen deadly formatting mistakes, clarifying the difference between a spec script and production script, and mastering the vital art of proofreading. For the first time, readers will find instructions for formatting instant messages, text messages, email exchanges and caller ID.

"Aspiring writers sometimes wonder why people don't want to read their scripts. Sometimes it's not their story. Sometimes the format distracts. To write a screenplay, you need to learn the science. And this is the best, simplest, easiest to read book to teach you that science. It's the one I recommend to my students at UCLA."

— Antwone Fisher, from the foreword

CHRISTOPHER RILEY is a professional screenwriter working in Hollywood with his wife and writing partner, Kathleen Riley. Together they wrote the 1999 theatrical feature *After the Truth*, a multiple-award-winning German language courtroom thriller. Since then, the husband-wife team has written scripts ranging from legal and political thrillers to action-romances for Touchstone Pictures, Paramount Pictures, Mandalay Television Pictures and Sean Connery's Fountainbridge Films.

In addition to writing, the Rileys train aspiring screenwriters for work in Hollywood and have taught in Los Angeles, Chicago, Washington D.C., New York, and Paris. From 2005 to 2008, the author directed the acclaimed Act One Writing Program in Hollywood.

$24.95 · 208 PAGES · ORDER NUMBER 130RLS · ISBN: 9781932907636

THE SCRIPT-SELLNG GAME - 2ND ED.
A HOLLYWOOD INSIDER'S LOOK AT GETTING YOUR SCRIPT SOLD AND PRODUCED

KATHIE FONG YONEDA

Kathie Fong Yoneda

Getting Your Script Sold and Produced 2nd Edition

The Script-Selling Game is about what they never taught you in film school. This is a look at screenwriting from the other side of the desk — from a buyer who wants to give writers the guidance and advice that will help them to not only elevate their craft but to also provide them with the down-in-the-trenches information of what is expected of them in the script selling marketplace.

It's like having a mentor in the business who answers your questions and provides you with not only valuable information, but real-life examples on how to maneuver your way through the Hollywood labyrinth. While the first edition focused mostly on film and television movies, the second edition includes a new chapter on animation and another on utilizing the Internet to market yourself and find new opportunities, plus an expansive section on submitting for television and cable.

"I've been writing screenplays for over 20 years. I thought I knew it all — until I read The Script-Selling Game. *The information in Kathie Fong Yoneda's fluid and fun book really enlightened me. It's an invaluable resource for any serious screenwriter."*

> — Michael Ajakwe Jr., Emmy-winning TV producer, *Talk Soup*; Executive Director of Los Angeles Web Series Festival (LAWEBFEST); and creator/ writer/director of *Who...* and *Africabby* (AjakweTV.com)

"Kathie Fong Yoneda knows the business of show from every angle and she generously shares her truly comprehensive knowledge — her chapter on the Web and new media is what people need to know! She speaks with the authority of one who's been there, done that, and gone on to put it all down on paper. A true insider's view."

> — Ellen Sandler, former co-executive producer of *Everybody Loves Raymond* and author of *The TV Writer's Workbook*

KATHIE FONG YONEDA has worked in film and television for more than 30 years. She has held executive positions at Disney, Touchstone, Disney TV Animation, Paramount Pictures Television, and Island Pictures, specializing in development and story analysis of both live-action and animation projects. Kathie is an internationally known seminar leader on screenwriting and development and has conducted workshops in France, Germany, Austria, Spain, Ireland, Great Britain, Australia, Indonesia, Thailand, Singapore, and throughout the U.S. and Canada.

$19.95 · 248 PAGES · ORDER NUMBER 161RLS · ISBN 13: 9781932907919

THE MYTH OF MWP

In a dark time, a light bringer came along, leading the curious and the frustrated to clarity and empowerment. It took the well-guarded secrets out of the hands of the few and made them available to all. It spread a spirit of openness and creative freedom, and built a storehouse of knowledge dedicated to the betterment of the arts.

The essence of the Michael Wiese Productions (MWP) is empowering people who have the burning desire to express themselves creatively. We help them realize their dreams by putting the tools in their hands. We demystify the sometimes secretive worlds of screenwriting, directing, acting, producing, film financing, and other media crafts.

By doing so, we hope to bring forth a realization of 'conscious media' which we define as being positively charged, emphasizing hope and affirming positive values like trust, cooperation, self-empowerment, freedom, and love. Grounded in the deep roots of myth, it aims to be healing both for those who make the art and those who encounter it. It hopes to be transformative for people, opening doors to new possibilities and pulling back veils to reveal hidden worlds.

MWP has built a storehouse of knowledge unequaled in the world, for no other publisher has so many titles on the media arts. Please visit www.mwp.com where you will find many free resources and a 25% discount on our books. Sign up and become part of the wider creative community!

Onward and upward,

Michael Wiese
Publisher/Filmmaker